MW01034715

COMING

AND

CRISIS ᴬᵀ CLOSE
THE

W. D. FRAZEE

1800-WDF-1840 / 706-820-9755
www.WDFsermons.org

A Department of Wildwood Sanitarium, Inc.
www.WildwoodHealth.org

Published in the USA

January, 2016

ISBN: 978-1-944501-02-0

COMING EVENTS

AND

CRISIS AT THE CLOSE

W. D. FRAZEE

WHO WAS W.D. FRAZEE?

It goes without saying that "a tall man casts a long shadow." And as the sun begins to set, the shadow grows even longer. W.D. Frazee (1906-1996) was educated in medical science at Loma Linda and in health evangelism by the legendary J.H.N. Tindall. In 1942, Elder Frazee and a faithful team of pioneers established Wildwood Sanitarium and Medical Missionary Institute where physicians, nurses, pastors, and laymen received practical training in medical evangelism.

From its humble beginnings, Wildwood has echoed the vision of the founders, nurtured in a prayerful study of the Scriptures and Spirit of Prophecy counsels. Today, it continues to educate medical missionary evangelistic workers from all over the world at its country outpost near Chattanooga, TN.

W. D. FRAZEE (1906-1996)

In 1985, during his retirement years, Elder Frazee established "Pioneers Memorial," which is now "W.D. Frazee Sermons". Thousands of audio files on various topics are distributed each year, and tens of thousands have gone around the world. We store, copy, and distribute the sermons of W.D. Frazee, E.A. Sutherland, Dr. Charles Thomas, and other pioneers of medical missionary work. Our goal is to remind this generation of the success and struggles of our self-supporting pioneers so that we may build on their experiences to finish the work in this generation.

You can view Elder Frazee's sermon titles available in audio and transcribed format on our website. We also have eBooks and many other special features on the site, including many free instant downloads. Visit us soon!

WDFsermons.org

CONTENTS

"As we near the close of this world's history, the prophecies relating to the last days especially demand our study." *Christ's Object Lessons*, p. 133.

Section 1 – Coming Events

INTRODUCTION

Understand, O son of man: for at the time of
the end shall be the vision. Daniel 8:17.

Moffatt renders it:
Understand the vision, O son of man: for
it relates to the crisis at the close.

What is this vision, and what is the crisis at the close? Before those questions are answered, here are several Bible texts which provide a bit of background.

In 1 Chronicles 12:32, we find that the men of Issachar were men that had understanding of the times to know what Israel ought to do. Does knowing what to do have any connection with knowing the time? Oh, yes. Suppose I wake up in the night not knowing what time it is. Do I know what to do? It may be time to get up. It may be time to turn over and go back to sleep. What do I do? I look at my watch. Otherwise, I might find myself coming down for breakfast at one o'clock in the morning. Or I might miss an appointment by going to sleep when it's time to get up.

We are told in *Testimonies for the Church*, Vol. 6, page 24: "It is the very essence of all right faith to do the right thing at the right time." The emphasis is on *knowing the time.*

> And that, knowing the time, that now it is high time to awake out of sleep: for now is our salvation nearer than when we believed. Romans 13:11.

Why does Paul say it is time to wake up? Because we know the time. Again and again that thought is emphasized. There are times we would like to know what God hasn't revealed. We are warned in Acts 1:7 that it is not for us to know the times and the seasons which the Father has put in His own power.

> The secret things belong unto the LORD our God: but those things which are revealed belong unto us and to our children for ever. Deuteronomy 29:29.

So the things we should study are the things which are revealed. When we study the subject of this chapter and this book, we should focus our attention on what God has clearly revealed, and avoid filling our minds with conjectures, speculations, and ideas of men concerning the things that God has not revealed. I don't know of anything that furnishes a more fertile field for human speculations than the future. But, thank God, the way we need to travel through the searchlight of prophecy is opened clear and plain. And we need not be as those that walk in darkness.

Jesus began to preach concerning His mission on the basis of the fulfillment of time prophecy. We are told that Jesus came into Galilee shortly after His baptism preaching the gospel of the kingdom and saying:

> The time is fulfilled, and the kingdom of God is at hand. Mark 1:15.

What time was Jesus talking about? What prophecy was He referring to? He was referring to that prophecy of our opening text — the wonderful prophecy of Daniel 8. It was that prophecy which clearly proves that our Lord Jesus is the true Messiah, the Anointed One of the Old Testament prophecies, for He came on time.

> But when the fulness of the time was come, God sent forth His Son, made of a woman, made under the law. Galatians 4:4.

The baptism of Jesus by John in the River Jordan occurred in the fall of the year A.D. 27. That was exactly the time that Daniel had foretold, being the end of the 483 years, the 69 weeks reaching from the decree to restore and to rebuild Jerusalem unto the Messiah the Prince. (Daniel 9:24-25) In B.C. 457, that decree to restore and rebuild Jerusalem went forth. Exactly 483 years later, in A.D. 27, Jesus was baptized. Having received the anointing of the Spirit, He went forth proclaiming Himself and His mission to be the fulfillment of that prophecy which had been given through Daniel over 500 years before. He knew the time. Those who listened to His message knew the time. Knowing the time, they knew what to do; they were prepared to welcome the Messiah.

It is true that they didn't fully understand all the events to take place in connection with the coming of the Messiah. They expected a kingdom of glory to be set up at that time. But, as we know, three and a half years later, the cross was set up on Golgotha, and our Lord Jesus died in the midst of that last week. That very event was such a bitter disappointment to His followers that, for the time being, practically all of them lost faith. But Jesus appeared to them after His resurrection and comforted them, instructing them in the Scriptures. He built their faith on the firm foundation, on the prophetic word. He returned to heaven, and those same disciples who were so bitterly disappointed were entrusted with the message to carry to the ends of the earth, which they did. And the gospel was preached to every creature under heaven in one generation. Such was the wonderful fulfillment of that prophecy which God had given in the 8th and 9th chapters of Daniel.

Note, however, that our opening text says that the vision of Daniel 8 relates primarily to the crisis at the close. When Daniel heard a certain one speaking, he heard a question asked:

> How long shall be the vision concerning the daily sacrifice, and the transgression of desolation, to give both the sanctuary and the host to be trodden under foot? Daniel 8:13.

In other words, how long would the powers of the earth, dominated and inspired by the devil, trample down God's sanctuary, God's people, His truth, and His saints? The answer came:

> And he said unto me, Unto two thousand and three hundred days; then shall the sanctuary be cleansed. Daniel 8:14.

There was to be something about the cleansing of the sanctuary which would have to do with victory for God's people, the vindication of God's government, and the final overthrow of all the enemies of God and His truth. Those 2300 *days*, of course, were symbolic, representing 2300 *years*. Ezekiel says:

> I have appointed thee each day for a year. Ezekiel 4:6.

Consequently, from that B.C. 457 date, we follow down prophetic time and focus on the year 1844 when those long 2300 years came to an end. What was so significant about the year 1844? What crisis correlates with that date? What is there about the cleansing of the sanctuary that has anything to do with that crisis? These are very important questions which will be answered in coming chapters. But let's now take a brief look at these problems.

Paul makes it clear in Hebrews 8 and 9 that the sanctuary is in heaven. The cleansing of the sanctuary is the blotting out of the sins of God's children from the record books above, at the close of the investigative judgment. But keep in mind that while the sanctuary is in heaven, God also has a sanctuary on earth. His people are called His temple, His sanctuary. And the blotting out of sins in the sanctuary in heaven is the bookkeeping record of the actual blotting out of the sins of God's people from their hearts and lives down here below. And God will never blot out the sins in the books up there unless they are blotted out down here. God will never have an angel make an inaccurate or false entry in the books of heaven. And when the sanctuary is cleansed up there, you may be sure that it is because the sanctuary is cleansed down here. Jesus is going to purify His church today as He purified the temple of Jerusalem at the beginning and ending of His ministry. And it is on that cleansing of the sanctuary, along with the great cleansing of the sanctuary in heaven, that we want to focus.

Revelation 14 contains the message for this judgment hour. When the time comes for the sanctuary in heaven to be cleansed, and for a cleansed people to be developed here in this world, three mighty angels will fly in the midst of heaven with a message to those who dwell on the earth. In verse 6 comes the angel that we speak of as the first angel.

Notice his message in verse 7:

> Saying with a loud voice, Fear God, and give glory to Him; for the hour of His judgment is come: and worship Him that made heaven, and earth, and the sea, and the fountains of waters. Revelation 14:7.

Here is a message which indeed relates to the crisis at the close — a message which is present truth in the judgment hour. And so, at the time that Jesus was about to enter that most holy place in heaven to cleanse the sanctuary, and to enter into the work of investigative judgment preparatory to the blotting out of those sins, this message must go to all the world — "Fear God, and give glory to Him; for the hour of His judgment is come." That message could be given only to this last generation.

Paul, in reasoning before Felix, spoke of righteousness and temperance and "judgment to come." Jesus pointed His hearers forward to the time when every idle word must be given account for in the day of judgment. But here, in Revelation 14, we have a message going to all the world, saying, not that the judgment *will* come but that the judgment *is* come. This message is the counterpart of the Daniel 8:14 prophecy. Daniel 8:14 gives us the *time*; Revelation 14:6-7 gives us the *message* for that time. The time is 1844, the time for the cleansing of the sanctuary in heaven and on earth. The message is Revelation 14:7, "Fear God, and give glory to Him; for the hour of His judgment is come: and worship Him that made heaven, and earth, and the sea, and the fountains of waters."

As the result of such a message, a group of people are pictured in the 12th verse. What kind of people are they?

> Here is the patience of the saints: here are they that keep the commandments of God, and the faith of Jesus. Revelation 14:12.

These people are ready for Jesus to come. The 14th verse presents Jesus coming on the clouds with a sharp sickle in His hand. And the angel says to the Saviour:

> Thrust in Thy sickle, and reap: for the time is come for Thee to reap; for the harvest of the earth is ripe. Revelation 14:15.

In Matthew 13:38, Jesus says that the good seed are the children of the kingdom. In verse 39, He says that the harvest is the end of the world. Then, at harvest time, with the crop fully mature, with God's children like Him in every way, Jesus comes. This is the message which draws those people out from every nation and kindred and tongue and people, and develops them and perfects them and presents them at the coming of Jesus "without fault before the throne of God." I want to be in that company, don't you? Knowing the time, we know that we have come to that hour. It is the prophetic time given us in Daniel 8 and 9 that shows us that we are in that hour. It can't be much longer. Jesus is finishing His work in heaven; He is finishing it on earth. And knowing the time, it is high time to wake out of sleep and share in these closing movements.

Note this carefully. Revelation 14 depicts a great struggle, a great issue. The first angel speaks positively of the true worship, but the second and third angels speak very definitely of the *false* worship. The second angel says:

> Babylon is fallen, is fallen, that great city, because she made all nations drink of the wine of the wrath of her fornication. Revelation 14:8.

Babylon represents today the great worldwide combination of error and falsehood — false religion claiming to speak for God but really speaking for Satan. Against that we are warned by this message. The third angel follows with a loud voice, saying:

> If any man worship the beast and his image, and receive his mark in his forehead, or in his hand, the same shall drink of the wine of the wrath of God. Revelation 14:9-10.

These judgments are coming upon those who worship the beast and his image, and on all who receive his mark. Here indeed is a crisis at the close. The beast and his image seek to enforce their mark upon the minds and consciences of men, and God warns us against that. That crisis is more fully pictured in Revelation 13 where the leopard beast that came from the sea is clearly presented. It is evident that the leopard beast is a symbol of the papacy, the great power that rules from the Vatican. We also know that following in the footsteps of the papacy is the image of the beast, which represents the power of apostate Protestantism, now developing, which will soon unite with old papal Rome in a persecution against the people of God to the point that:

> ... no man might buy or sell, save he that had the mark, or the name of the beast, or the number of his name. Revelation 13:17.

Will that be a crisis? Yes, that is the crisis at the close. And there will be a death decree:

> ... the image of the beast should both speak, and cause that as many as would not worship the image of the beast should be killed. Revelation 13:15.

Do you see that all hell is moved against the development of the people who keep the commandments of God and the faith of Jesus? This is indeed a crisis — a crisis in the government of God, and a crisis in the government of hell. This vision relates to the crisis at the close — the crisis just before Jesus comes — and every soul in this world will either be one of that little company who keeps the commandments of God and the faith of Jesus, or they will be numbered among those who worship the beast and his image and receive his mark in their right hands or in their foreheads. Have we truly come to grips with that crisis? We have often been told that it's typically true that trouble is greater in anticipation than it is in reality. But we're also told that this is not true concerning the time of trouble ahead.

The most vivid presentation, according to *Great Controversy*, page 622, cannot equal the magnitude of the ordeal through which we must pass. All hell will be turned loose to prevent the development of that group of people who have the seal of God in their foreheads, who keep the commandments of God, and whose sins are blotted out. The devil does not want a clean sanctuary. He does not want a clean heart in any soul. He does not want a clean church. He does not want sin to be eliminated and put away forever. No, the devil doesn't want that. He is going to do everything he can to prevent it.

Do we know anything about the sequence and order of the events in this last battle? Of course we do. There are some things we don't know. If you were in God's place, which ones would you reveal to God's people — the things they need to know or just the things they would like to know? Occasionally, somebody asks me a question concerning coming events, and the answer I have to give is, "I don't know." But we aren't completely ignorant about the future. We can know all we need to know, and we need to know all we can know.

When Jesus was on earth, fulfilling prophecy and calling attention to the fulfillment of prophecy, hundreds of His followers were bitterly disappointed. Although Christ's crucifixion was an exact fulfillment of prophecy, His followers lost hope when they saw Him hanging on the cross. Why? They had not fully studied the prophecies. Their minds were filled with the traditions of the religious leaders of that time. Christ's disciples thought they knew the Bible. In fact, the 12 apostles were ordained ministers of Jesus Christ. But they were bitterly disappointed and lost hope when the Lamb of God was slain on Calvary. You and I look back at it now and wonder why they couldn't see it.

Here is an interesting quote concerning them and us. It's in *Great Controversy*, page 594: "Before His crucifixion the Saviour explained to His disciples that He was to be put to death and to rise again from the tomb, and angels were present to impress His words on minds and hearts. But the disciples were looking for temporal deliverance from the Roman yoke, and they could not tolerate the thought that He in whom all their hopes centered should suffer an ignominious death. The words which they needed to remember were banished from their minds; and when the time of trial came, it found them unprepared. The death of Jesus as fully destroyed their hopes as if He had not forewarned them. So in the prophecies the future is opened before us as plainly as it was opened to the disciples by the words of Christ. The events connected with the close of probation and the work of preparation for the time of trouble, are clearly presented. But multitudes have no more understanding of these important truths than if they had never been revealed."

Multitudes today are going to be surprised by the coming events when they *could* know all they need to know — all that has any bearing on their preparation. The last quotation speaks about the close of probation and the work of preparation for the time of trouble. Does the close of probation take place *before* the coming of Jesus, *at* the coming of Jesus, or *after* the coming of Jesus? All three of those stands are being taught in the world today. They can't all be correct. Which one is *true*? Does it make any difference? Absolutely. Knowing the time, we know what to do.

Does the time of trouble occur *before* or *after* the coming of Jesus? Does it come *before* the close of probation or *after* it? All those different positions are being taught by various churches in the world today, and all claim to teach out of the Bible. They can't all be right. Do you know which one of *those* is correct? Do you know how to *prove* it? What the angel said relates to the crisis at the close. Let's see what Jesus said about the prophecy of Daniel:

> When ye therefore shall see the abomination of desolation, spoken of by Daniel the prophet, stand in the holy place, (whoso readeth, let him understand:) Then let them which be in Judaea flee into the mountains. Matthew 24:15-16.

In Luke, we get a clearer idea of what Jesus meant:

> And when ye shall see Jerusalem compassed with armies, then know that the desolation thereof is nigh. Then let them which are in Judaea flee to the mountains; and let them which are in the midst of it depart out; and let not them that are in the countries enter thereinto. Luke 21:20-21.

When those Roman armies came against Jerusalem nearly 40 years after Jesus spoke these words, the Christians who had remembered and cherished the words of Christ saw in that approach of the Romans the sign that they should flee to the mountains. Why? Because Jesus said that when they saw that sign then they should know that the desolation thereof is nigh.

The Roman army under Cestius came and encamped around the city and laid siege to it. But just at the moment when it seemed that the Jews must surrender, Cestius, for no reason in the world, started a retreat to the sea; and the Jews, sallying forth after him, left the gates open; and the Christians, remembering the sign that Jesus had given, fled.

Someone might have said, "What is the use of fleeing now? The Romans are gone." But Jesus had told them that when they saw those armies around Jerusalem then know that her desolation was nigh. They knew it. They knew the time. They knew the signal. They acted; they fled to the mountains. It wasn't long before the Roman army, under Titus, came back. This time it came quickly by forced marches. A great army surrounded the city. And before that siege was over, one million Jews perished by crucifixion, starvation, inner conflicts within the city, and many other ways. In the fate of that city, we may behold the doom of the world. But not one Christian perished in the siege of that city. And not one of God's children upon whom is the seal of God is going to perish in the doom of this world. Not one. Why? Because they know the time, they watch the prophetic signals, and they move under the leadership of Jesus. We need to know what is soon coming to pass, and we need to know the signals.

As far as dates are concerned, the last prophetic date is 1844. At that time, the angel took his place, with one foot on the land and one on the sea, and with his right hand to heaven swore that there should be prophetic time no longer. Why? Because God's prophetic clock had struck the hour of the final movements. From 1844 on, it is not a matter of days or weeks or months or years but, rather, a development of a people. And when those people are developed, when their characters are perfected, then the crisis at the close breaks with all the force of a great hurricane or tornado. There is something which is about to take place which inspiration has said is to be to us a sign just as definite and clear and plain as was the Roman armies around Jerusalem. And there are some things that we're to know when we see that happening. This is what we need to be studying.

People today are spending so much time trying to keep up with current events. They have the newspaper, radio, television, and other ways of keeping up. But every one of those means can tell you something only *after* it has happened. Anything else is merely human guesswork and speculation, liable to error of all kinds. Even the reporting of the news is sometimes tainted, whether accidentally or on purpose. But in the Bible and the Spirit of Prophecy, the events are revealed *before* they come to pass! Isn't it a pity that multitudes are paying no more attention to these prophecies than if they had never been written? The prophecies are the timetables, the "schedule of events" with which you and I want to be familiarizing our minds. We want to have them so fixed in our minds, that if perchance in some lonely cell we are left without our Bibles in print, we shall have so much stored away in our memories that we shall suffer no loss because of the lack of the printed Word. Let's fill our minds with Daniel and Revelation. Let's know the events that are coming to pass.

Someone may say, "Oh, I already know what is coming." But we must not be too confident. As we study further, we may find that some things that we thought were so, aren't so. Or we may learn some things that we didn't previously know. I would rather know five things about coming events, and know them well, than to know ten things and be hazy and uncertain and incorrect. We must learn what is true and be able to recognize what isn't.

How many messages are there in Revelation 14? Three! The work of those messages is to get people ready. Are they getting you ready? In the Spirit of Prophecy, these three messages are presented as three steps. In the first vision that was given the servant of the Lord, she saw a narrow path cast high above the world (see *Early Writings*, page 14). The three steps are at the beginning of that path; they are the first, second, and third messages. We need to know exactly what those three messages are, when they rose, what they did for the people in the 1800s, and what they are designed to do for us today. If we allow these messages to do their work, to speak to our hearts, and we listen and do something about them, we shall be among those who are pictured in the latter part of Revelation 14 — golden grain, ready to be gathered for the kingdom of God, a people who are without fault, who keep the commandments of God and the faith of Jesus.

The only thing which can cleanse the sanctuary in heaven or earth is the blood of Jesus Christ.

Without shedding of blood is no remission. Hebrews 9:22.

The reason that these people who are developed by this three-fold message are ready to meet the Saviour is that they have yielded their hearts and lives fully to the cleansing power of that blood. They have allowed it to do a completed work. Therefore a great program of education goes with this message to point out sin, exalting the law of God, that we may know what is wrong and put it away. But never think that by our human efforts alone we shall arrive either at an understanding of His will completely, or a complete cleansing from the sins that light brings to view. The angel who flies in the heavens has the everlasting gospel to preach unto them that dwell on the earth, the gospel that in Adam and Enoch and Noah's day brought comfort to those hearts that were bowed down under the weight of sin, the gospel that the Holy Spirit preached before unto Abraham and to Moses, and the everlasting gospel that Jesus preached, is being heralded today, pointing men and women to the cross of Christ as the place where sin may be repented of.

Knowing the time, we must wake out of sleep and hasten to get that work done. Knowing the time, we realize that we have little time left to prepare. Knowing the time, we shall want to be quick in our movements. So I trust that the Spirit of God may speak to our hearts right now. If sin is discovered by the searchlight of the Spirit in the heart, let us put it away and claim the covering blood of Jesus so that we may be under the shadow of the Almighty, protected by the covering righteousness of Christ.

THREE ANGELS' MESSAGES

*These messages were represented to me as an anchor
to the people of God. Those who understand and
receive them will be kept from being swept away by
the many delusions of Satan. Early Writings, p. 256.*

The first, second, and third angel's messages are not only a firm platform of three steps, but they are an anchor. If understood and received, this three-pointed anchor will keep us from being tossed about in the waves of the devil's delusions.

In the previous chapter, we introduced these three messages and showed that they relate to the last generation. How would you prove from the Bible that this message relates to the last people upon earth? Revelation 14:14 pictures the Son of God coming in the clouds of heaven to harvest the earth as soon as the message is given. Also, the seventh verse announces that the hour of His judgment is come. Men cannot be judged until they have lived, because they are judged according to their works.

This is clear in Revelation chapter 20:

> And I saw the dead, small and great, stand before God; and the books were opened: and another book was opened, which is the book of life: and the dead were judged out of those things which were written in the books, according to their works. Revelation 20:12.

So while the judgment can begin while men are still living on earth, it must continue down to the time immediately before the coming of Jesus.

Let's examine the three messages from two different standpoints. First, let's study them as they came to us historically, clustering around 1844. Then we'll look at them as they locate certain specific events and periods, some of which are still future. It's always interesting to notice how much God can pack into a few verses or even just a few words. And there is a great deal wrapped in Revelation 14.

To review briefly, this judgment hour of the first angel points to what time? 1844. What time in 1844? October 22, the fall of the year. The great 2300-day prophecy of Daniel 8:14 came to an end on October 22, 1844, and Jesus began the work of the investigative judgment in connection with the cleansing of the sanctuary.

The people who gave the message, "The hour of His judgment is come," and pointed out October 22, 1844 as the time for it, thought that Jesus was coming back to earth on that day. They thought the judgment that would take place was at the time when all nations are gathered before Him and He separates the sheep from the goats, and punishments and rewards are given. Did that take place at that time? No, but a preliminary phase of judgment took place. That was the investigative judgment to determine the rewards and punishments. Does the Bible indicate that those punishments and rewards are all arranged before Christ appears? Yes. In Revelation 22, after the announcement that the unjust remain unjust and that the righteous remain righteous, Jesus says:

> And, behold, I come quickly; and My reward is with Me, to give every man according as his work shall be. Revelation 22:12.

Are there rewards with Him when He comes? Yes, meaning that whatever investigation to be done — the investigative judgment — is completed before He appears. But back in 1844, people did not understand this.

All over the world, literally dozens of people, each one for a time unknown to each other, studied the prophecies of Daniel and Revelation, and dozens of them came to the conclusion that the prophecies would run out and Christ would come around the year 1844. God was stirring up the minds of many different people in many parts of the world to study these prophecies. Who led out in America? William Miller. There were others who joined him, and soon there were several hundred ministers of various denominations giving this message. Keep in mind what they were preaching — that Christ was coming immediately. They knew nothing about the sanctuary or the investigative judgment. They were not preaching the Sabbath. And, except for certain ones who came in toward the end, they were not preaching the state of the dead. Of course, they didn't have the Spirit of Prophecy. The great central truth that they were teaching and preaching was the coming of Christ. That was the great truth that God wanted the whole world stirred with, and that was what they understand this message to mean:

> Fear God and give glory to Him, for the hour of His judgment is come. Revelation 14:7.

Does the coming of the judgment include the coming of the Judge to this world? Yes, just as when the disciples preached that the kingdom of heaven was at hand. That, in a sense, includes the setting up of the entire kingdom of God, and will not have its complete fulfillment until this whole earth is made new as it was in Eden. But, there were certain things that must be done. Must Jesus die upon the cross before that kingdom of glory could ever be ushered in? Yes, but they didn't see that at first. They came to see it later.

In 1844, it was preached that the coming of Jesus was near, even at the door. It is interesting to notice what signs Jesus gave right at that time to stir their hearts. Along with the prophecies of Daniel and Revelation, He gave them signs in the heavens. What were those signs? One was the dark day of May 19, 1780. The moon darkened the following night. Then the great shower of stars on November, 13, 1833. There were thousands of people who saw those signs. And as Miller and the Advent preachers came with their tents, charts, and leaflets, they called attention to the fact that the prophecies of Daniel had been fulfilled, and the beast had come and gone, and the papal reign had expired in 1798, and the signs in the heavens had come. You can see that the people had ample reason to be stirred and to believe just exactly as Jesus said:

> When you see all these things, know that it is near, even at the door. Matthew 24:33.

There were thousands of God's people in America and over in England and the continent of Europe who accepted the Advent message and who looked for Jesus to come shortly. God never intended for time to go on and on after 1844. He intended that the judgment which began October 22, 1844, was to usher in the last scenes in short order. It could have been. We're plainly told that if all who gave the first and second angel's messages had united in accepting and giving the third, that the world would have quickly been warned, and Jesus would have come long ago. Those words are a challenge to us. They will help us to understand the meaning of some of these statements that we read from time to time.

God was giving the message the way He wanted it given. He was ready for the final work, and it was essential that His people wake up and get ready. Due to an error in calculation, they first expected the Saviour to come in the spring of 1844. A disappointment ensued when He didn't come. For some weeks, there was a discouragement that came upon the waiting ones. But, in the summer of 1844, light came to the Advent band on the true reckoning of the prophetic periods, pointing out that the 2300 days would not run out until the *fall* of 1844. This focused attention especially upon October 22. (Note: If you are not familiar with these historical events, you can read about them in *Great Controversy* in the chapter "Prophecies Fulfilled.")

During the summer of 1844, they came to realize that their position had been foretold and described by Christ in the parable of the ten virgins — that while the bridegroom tarried, they all slumbered and slept. They applied this parable to the time between the spring and autumn of 1844. They reasoned: a prophetic day is a literal year. So half of a 24-hour day would be six months, and that's where they were between the spring and fall of 1844. Half of that would be midnight, the summer of 1844. In the parable, at midnight there was a cry made, "Behold the bridegroom cometh," which would correspond to the 22nd of October, 1844.

The message swelled into a great cry, like a tornado, sweeping from town to town, from city to city, and from state to state. It was a wonderful time. And it is marvelous how much they did in just a few weeks. Thousands were converted, and there were anywhere from 50,000-100,000 people who were confidently expecting Jesus to come on October 22, 1844.

Following the first message, what does the second angel say?

Babylon is fallen, is fallen. Revelation 14:8.

The people gave this message particularly in the summer of 1844, and it came to pass in this way. During the early part of the preaching of the first message, in the 1830s and the 1840s, many of the Protestant churches opened their doors to the preaching of the message; in fact, that is where it was preached. William Miller had no thought of starting another church; neither did Himes, Litch, Storrs, White, Bates, or the others. They thought Jesus was coming right away, and they thought that everybody in every church would be glad to know it and get ready. But, as the message gained in power, it brought more and more separation in spirit between those who fully accepted it and those who fully rejected it. It's hard for light and darkness to have communion. It is hard for Christ and Belial to have fellowship (2 Corinthians 6:15).

On top of this, there was the disappointment after expecting Jesus to come. That gave those in the churches who were not in favor of the message a good excuse for rejecting it. They said, "You were mistaken, weren't you? You had better forget all that kind of talk, and come back and be normal." But the others kept studying the prophecies and came up with another date. Many of the leaders in the popular churches turned against that proclamation. So during the summer of 1844, there arose a great deal of opposition in the churches against the Advent message. On the other hand, within the Advent movement there arose the cry of the second angel, "Babylon is fallen, is fallen." They applied the term "Babylon" to the confused state of organized religion. There were those who gave the message with mighty power to come out of such confusion. Some of them *had* to come out. Hundreds were disfellowshipped from those popular churches because they clung to the Advent faith.

In the summer and fall of 1844, there were three different messages spreading all at once.

The first angel's message said:

> ... the hour of His judgment is come. Revelation 14:7.

The people were preaching that with great power, pointing to October 22, 1844. Besides that, they were preaching the midnight cry:

> Behold, the bridegroom cometh; go ye out to meet him. Matthew 25:6.

And the second angel's message which said,

> Babylon is fallen, is fallen... Revelation 14:8.

and

> Come out of her, my people. Revelation 18:4.

Those were the messages that were spreading in one great sweep of glory in the summer and fall of 1844. Many united in the movement, and great power went with it. It brought a separation from the world, a separation from the popular churches, and a fitting up for heaven. Believers confessed their faults; they made things right. They quit bickering and quarrelling, setting aside everything that would come between them and God. And they came to October 22 with hearts humbled and penitent, trusting in the righteousness of Jesus, and expecting all that day for the Saviour to come. Of course, He didn't come. That is, He didn't come to the *world*. Where *did* He come? He entered into the most holy place in the heavenly sanctuary. He came where He had the appointment.

Isn't it sad that nobody here in this world was looking for Him where He was? Similarly, when He had gone to the cross, that was the last place the disciples expected to find Him on that spring day of the Passover season. Where did they expect to see Him? On the throne. The Sunday before, they had marched in that triumphal procession with Jesus seated on a colt, while onlookers spread the palm branches and garments, waving their hands and waving palm branches and telling each other that Jesus was coming as the King of Israel. But within a few days, He was hanging upon a cross. Was that, in a true sense, the setting up of the kingdom? Yes. Without that, there could be no kingdom in which you and I could share. And so it was in 1844, when Jesus came to the most holy place; He came where He must come if there was to be any kingdom. Before Jesus can come and claim His people, what must happen to their sins? They must be blotted out. And that work had not been done. The investigative judgment must precede it.

When the judgment began, everybody who had expected Jesus to come that day went to bed that night disappointed. But the next morning, the Lord gave Hiram Edson a conviction. Heaven was open to his view. There in his cornfield, he saw clearly that our Great High Priest had the day before passed from the holy place to the most holy place to begin the work there which would culminate in His coming forth to bless His people. Hiram Edson communicated that conviction to others, and they began to study the Bible along that line. Light came from heaven.

A few days later, in South Portland, Maine, the Spirit of God came upon Ellen Harmon, and she was given a vision of the Advent people traveling the narrow path to the city of God. Not long afterwards, she was given a view of the passing of Jesus from the holy place to the most holy place. That was given in February of 1845. You will find it in *Early Writings* in the chapter called "End of the 2300 Days."

Not long after this, Joseph Bates was led to see the importance of the Seventh-day Sabbath. Within a few years, those who had the light from the Spirit of Prophecy in Maine, those who were keeping the Sabbath in New Hampshire and in Massachusetts, and those who had the light on the sanctuary out in New York were led together; and together they laid the foundation of this movement. What did they discover as they studied Revelation 14 that bore upon their disappointment? They discovered, first of all, that the hour of God's judgment pointed not to the coming of Jesus in the clouds of heaven, but to the beginning of *the investigative judgment* in heaven. Thus, they got the key to the unlocking of the mystery of their disappointment.

Also, as they looked in the open door of the most holy place, they saw an ark. What was in the ark? The law. And what did they find in that law? The fourth commandment. They saw the law as the standard of judgment; they saw that, here on earth, a company of people were to be developed in whose hearts that law would be written. They recognized that, in the third message, this company was brought to view:

> Here is the patience of the saints: here are they that keep the commandments of God, and the faith of Jesus. Revelation 14:12.

Could they then see a reason why Jesus didn't come on the 22nd of October? Could they see that a people had to be developed in whose hearts the law is fully written, and in whose lives the law is fully exemplified? Is that still true? Are we still waiting, and is the universe still waiting for the development of that people? That's the point. That is the work of this message — to develop that people in whose hearts the law of God is fully written, and in whose lives the law is fully lived. So, the third message unlocked their disappointment. It showed that Jesus had done just what He said He would do; He had appeared before the Ancient of Days in the most holy place to engage in the investigative judgment preparatory to blotting out the sins of His people. And while that work was going on in heaven, there must be a work of preparation among His people here on earth. As they studied, they saw that the Sabbath was the seal of that law. They recognized that, in the first message, the Sabbath was presented in principle because the first angel not only said:

Fear God, and give glory to Him;

but also said:

... worship Him that made heaven, and earth, and the sea, and the fountains of waters. Revelation 14:7.

Which commandment of the ten deals with that creative act of God? The fourth. And what is the sign of our worship of the One who made heaven and earth? Keeping the fourth commandment. So you see that the Sabbath truth is inherent in the first message. After the disappointment, the believers came to look at the message they had been giving, and they saw that the Sabbath reform was needed.

It is interesting to show how all the reforms of this message are inherent in that first message. Consider health reform, for example. If I think of God as Creator of all things, I think of Him as the One who gave *me* life. But He not only gave me life *historically*; He gives me life *daily*. He is the life-*giver*. He is working to build up my body. Who is working to tear it down? Satan. If I am worshiping Christ as Creator, will I work with Him to build up my body, or will I work with the enemy to tear it down? Would it be a good thing to study physiology to know how to cooperate with the Creator? Would that knowledge lead me to an understanding of the laws of health? And if I am really worshiping Him, what will I do when I understand those laws of life and health? I will follow them. I couldn't say that I worship Him as Creator and then try to tear down the thing that He created. So we see that health reform is inherent in that very first message of Revelation 14.

I have sketched briefly the historical development of the three messages. The first message began to be preached by William Miller in 1831, and it reached its climax in 1844. Is it still being given? Is it still true that the hour of His judgment is come, and that man should worship the Creator? Of course.

The second message was preached especially in the summer of 1844:

Babylon is fallen ... Revelation 14:8.

Is that still true? It is *increasingly* true. Babylon has fallen far lower than it was in 1844. So that is present truth right up until the time when Jesus comes.

The third message began to be preached after the disappointment of 1844, but is it still present truth?

Here is the patience of the saints: here are they that keep the commandments of God, and the faith of Jesus. Revelation 14:12.

Is God still calling for a people who keep the commandments of God and the faith of Jesus? Yes. And the people who are brought to view will be here in this world right up until the time that Jesus appears in the clouds. Every passing day makes it all the more true. So when we think of the three messages, we want to remember that these three steps are the three layers of a platform which runs all the way through to the coming of Jesus.

The first message that began back in 1831 by the preaching of William Miller continues to the coming of Jesus. The second message that was preached in the summer of 1844 never ceases to be true; Babylon will remain fallen until Christ comes. And the third message that began with Jesus' work in the most holy place also continues through. Thus we have a firm platform — as the Spirit of Prophecy calls it — the first, second, and third angels' messages. And when we see what they were given back in those days, we must never get the idea that it is something that happened only back *then*.

To clarify with a *contrast*, let me point out a message that came to the world before the flood. Who gave that message? Noah. How long was it given? For 120 years. Is that message still being given? No. It ceased to be given when Noah went into the ark. It had done its work. It was over. And we're not telling people today that God is going to destroy the world by a flood. If we did, we would be false prophets. We can think of other messages that were given at certain times. But here are messages that began back then — 1831, 1844, and thereafter — which continue down to our day. We are to think of them chronologically in their beginning, but we're to understand that they increase in power and application as time goes on.

The first angel's message:

> Saying with a loud voice, Fear God, and give glory to Him; for the hour of His judgment is come: and worship Him that made heaven, and earth, and the sea, and the fountains of waters. Revelation 14:7.

The hour of His judgment is come. Does that point to any particular time? Yes. What time? October 22, 1844 — the hour of His judgment. Does the judgment last more than a minute? Yes, it occupies a period of time. The clock struck the hour on October 22, 1844. How long does that hour last? We don't know the answer by the calendar. There is a work that is assigned, but the hour of God's judgment is not finished until the judgment is concluded. Are we still in that time? Yes. Let us think, then, of these two times as we look at that expression in the first message. We think of a specific date — October 22, 1844. We think also of the period of time reaching from October 22, 1844 on down to the completion of the judgment work, whenever that shall be. We are in that time. Is it important to know that? Why, it makes all the difference in the world, to know that we're in the judgment hour. Do we need to know the particular work and duties that pertain to this hour? Back in the days of Israel, when the high priest was in the sanctuary, did the people have different duties on the Day of Atonement? Yes. So today, in this judgment hour, the great purpose of life is to develop a people who will pass the judgment.

Now the second message:

> And there followed another angel, saying, Babylon is fallen, is fallen, that great city, because she made all nations drink of the wine of the wrath of her fornication. Revelation 14:8.

We have already seen that this message came in at the proper time chronologically. The Spirit of Prophecy plainly states that the first message was given at the right time, and the second message was given at the right time. But has Babylon's fall been completed? No. The only time one can say a fall is complete is when something can't fall any further. That is the point of the expression, "Babylon is fallen, is fallen."

> The second angel's message of Revelation 14 was first preached in the summer of 1844, and it then had a more direct application to the churches of the United States, where the warning of the judgment had been most widely proclaimed and most generally rejected, and where the declension in the churches had been most rapid. *Great Controversy*, p. 389.

Notice that it was the rejection of the first angel's message that made it necessary for the second angel to come and say, "Babylon is fallen, is fallen." Whenever individuals or churches or nations reject a message of light, they fall. But the fall was not complete in 1844.

> The churches then experienced a moral fall, in consequence of their refusal of the light of the Advent message; but that fall was not complete. As they have continued to reject the special truths for this time they have fallen lower and lower. *Ibid.*

Think of how evolution, modernism, and worldliness have crept in. The second message, while it began to be sounded back in the summer of 1844, finds its complete fulfillment only as we come to the time of complete apostasy in the popular churches. That apostasy, of course, is going to reach its climax in the image to the beast. Back in the days of the apostles, there was a mystery of iniquity already working that finally developed into the papacy — the antichrist, the beast. Today, that same spirit of apostasy is working and will finally bring to view an image to the beast. The third angel's message warns against it. So the image to the beast and the complete fall of Babylon come together. Do we have the image to the beast yet? No. Where will it be formed? In North America. And what will be the focal point of that movement represented by the image to the beast? The National Sunday Law. And that is called in prophecy "the mark." When the National Sunday Law will be enforced, it will be the enforcement of the mark of the beast. Does the third angel say anything about that? Yes.

> And the third angel followed them, saying with a loud voice, If any man worship the beast and his image, and receive his mark in his forehead, or in his hand, The same shall drink of the wine of the wrath of God. Revelation 14:9-10.

Have we come to that time yet? No. The third angel is pointing to a specific event, a specific time. It is the time of the forcing of the "mark of the beast" upon the people. And when we read Revelation 14, verses 9 and 10, we are thinking of something still future — the enforcement of the National Sunday Law in this country. What gives us light on that? The third angel's message. What warns us of that approaching test? The third angel's message. Does anyone receive the mark of the beast in the sense of the prophecy until this happens? No, it is still future. That same third angel's message says, "If any man worship the beast and his image,..." Is there any image today? No. But steps are being taken leading toward it. What will make the image? The union of church and state. On what issue are they going to unite? The Sunday Law. This issue marks the setting up of the image. But in that union of church and state, Babylon will have committed fornication with the kings of the earth, the governments of the earth, in a universal way that has not formerly been done.

The union of church and state has already been a reality in Europe in the Middle Ages, but America has been kept from such union. But when this country unites with the papacy in the enforcement of the false sabbath, the exalting of Sunday, then the fall of Babylon will be complete. We have, in this event, three things that the three angel's messages are dealing with — the complete fall of Babylon, the setting up of the image, and the enforcement of the mark. The purpose is to take people so far away from Jesus that they lose His image entirely and receive the mark of the beast. As expressed in the third angel's message, those who receive this mark will receive the wrath of God poured out full strength. When is that? The seven last plagues. How do we prove that?

> And I saw another sign in heaven, great and marvellous, seven angels having the seven last plagues; for in them is filled up the wrath of God. Revelation 15:1.

Is that past, present, or future? That is future. And they are foretold by the third angel.

What is the Loud Cry message?

> Come out of her, my people, that ye be not partakers of her sins, and that ye receive not of her plagues. For her sins have reached unto heaven, and God hath remembered her iniquities. Revelation 18:4-5.

The plagues immediately follow the message. Remember the story of Lot? Just before Sodom was destroyed, two angels came there and pulled anyone out that they could persuade to go with them. What happened to all the rest? The plagues of God were poured out upon Sodom, and all perished. So in our day, God is trying to pull His people out of Babylon before the seven plagues fall.

The three angels' messages deal with specific events and periods from 1844 to the coming of Jesus. And nobody can fully understand the three messages unless he has a clear view of the events. But without the messages of the three angels, the mere knowledge of these events is not of very great importance. The three messages not only point out the events and periods, they tell us what to *do* about them. They bring to view a work of reform, a changing of mind and heart and character. They call our attention from the false worship of men and devils to the true worship of Jesus and His Father in the sanctuary above. They call our attention from the mark of the beast to the seal of God. They call our attention from being made like the beast to being made like Christ. And everybody, according to the 14th chapter of Revelation, is soon going to be either with *Jesus* in mind and character or with the *beast* and his image, having his mark.

The light *accepted* will develop those who receive the seal of *God*; the light *rejected* will develop those who receive the mark of the *beast*. We are up against a great struggle. An hour of temptation and anguish begins with the National Sunday Law and continues to the opening of the seventh plague. That is the final conflict, from the setting up of the image and the enforcement of the mark, down to the glorification of the people at the time when the death decree is about to be enforced. The hour that you and I need to get our attention fixed upon is this time of the setting up of the image, to the jubilee when the saints of God are glorified and no more will ever feel the temptations of Satan.

> Their only hope of eternal life is to remain steadfast. Although their lives are at stake, they must hold fast the truth. *Early Writings*, p. 254.

Let's look up through the open heavens. Let's see Jesus standing there before the ark making His final intercession. And let's let Him blot out all our sins and write His law on our hearts, so that as we meet the beast and his image we will be triumphant because the law of love has been written in our very souls.

NATIONAL SUNDAY LAW

The great threefold message of Revelation 14 is meant to present the truths which will prepare a people for the coming of Jesus. These are the saints who keep the commandments of God and the faith of Jesus. This same group is brought to view in Revelation chapter 12. Notice what they are to experience:

> And the dragon was wroth with the woman, and went to make war with the remnant of her seed, which keep the commandments of God, and have the testimony of Jesus Christ. Revelation 12:17.

What will be the experience of those who keep all the commandments of God and have the testimony of Jesus? They will have a war on their hands. Who will be making that war? The dragon. The devil has always fought against the church. That has been true from the days of Adam and Eve down through time. There must be something special about this closing experience. This is a special war in this age-long controversy.

This verse is applied to the time just ahead of us. Chapter 36 of *Great Controversy* is titled "The Impending Conflict" and speaks of the National Sunday Law that marks the beginning of the enforcement of the mark of the beast:

> The dignitaries of church and state will unite to bribe, persuade, or compel all classes to honor the Sunday.... And even in free America, rulers and legislators, in order to secure public favor, will yield to the popular demand for a law enforcing Sunday observance. *Great Controversy*, p. 592.

This paragraph applies that to the soon-coming conflict, and it links it with the passing of the Sunday Law. This could be called the "opening gun" of the war. It will be no sneak attack. It will not come without agitation and publicity. We are told that the way it will come to pass is that the legislators will yield to the popular demand for a law enforcing Sunday observance.

So what will there be on the part of the public before that law is brought in? A *demand* for it from the *people*. And that is represented in Revelation 13. Revelation 12:17 is applied directly to that time. We may think we have problems now, and that we have conflicts. We do, but those are preliminary. The real war of Revelation 12:17 centers around the issue when the National Sunday Law is enforced.

> In the near future we shall see these words fulfilled as the Protestant churches unite with the world and with the papal power against commandment keepers. *Testimonies for the Church*, Vol. 5, p. 449.

The National Sunday Law is a great landmark. It stands out as something that can be seen. We have two expressions which indicate that it is a definite sign. Notice what it signifies:

> To secure popularity and patronage, legislators will yield to the demand for a Sunday Law. *Testimonies for the Church*, Vol. 5, p. 450.

Obviously, peer pressure is not merely a problem of youth. God's people, however, need not succumb to it.

> Those who fear God cannot accept an institution that violates a precept of the Decalogue. On this battlefield comes the last great conflict of the controversy between truth and error. *Ibid.*

What is one result of such a decree?

> By the decree enforcing the institution of the papacy in violation of the law of God, our nation will disconnect herself fully from righteousness. *Ibid.*, p. 451.

The National Sunday Law marks the end of our *nation's* probation, but not that of *individuals*. There was a time when the Jews filled up their cup of iniquity and sealed their national doom. Was it still possible for *individual* Jews to be saved? Oh, yes. But Israel as a nation filled up her cup of iniquity when she rejected Jesus and nailed Him to the cross. Israel's day as a nation was done, but *individuals* can still be saved.

We are almost at the end, but we are ready for the time of the marvelous working of Satan when we come to the decree enforcing the institution of the papacy, the Sunday Law.

As the approach of the Roman armies was a sign to the disciples of the impending destruction of Jerusalem, so may this apostasy be a sign to us that the limit of God's forbearance is reached, that the measure of our nation's iniquity is full, and that the angel of mercy is about to take her flight, never to return. *Ibid.*

There is a very fine point here. There is a difference between the National Sunday Law and the close of probation. When the National Sunday Law is passed, it is a sign to us that the angel of mercy is about to take her flight, never to return. It doesn't say that she *has* taken her flight. There is still mercy, but not for long. What will have happened? National apostasy will have filled up the cup of iniquity. Our nation will have disconnected herself fully from righteousness by the National Sunday Law. That is national apostasy. That is the setting up of the image. And, in that, our nation will align herself fully with the dragon and the beast. Thus, the threefold union will be complete.

If the cup of our nation's iniquity is then full, why does probation not close at the time of the National Sunday Law? When Sodom was about to be destroyed, God sent two angels to that city. An opportunity was given for people to reveal their character, which they did; opportunity was given for people to escape, and some did. But even when Sodom had sealed its doom and was ripe for destruction, God through His angel warned Lot to hasten and flee the city, because nothing could be done to it until he was out. Similarly today, God is ready to pour out His judgments upon this nation and upon Babylon as soon as this threefold union is complete. But God has a people in Babylon. So, before He pours out the plagues, He sends the message which says, "Come out of her, my people." The only purpose of the time between the National Sunday Law and the close of probation is to get God's people out of Babylon — out of the Sunday-keeping churches — and into the remnant church.

The decision on the part of our nation is final, irrevocable, and irreversible. It will never turn back once it has gone over the precipice with the devil. This nation will have disconnected itself fully from righteousness. That is why we should give earnest warnings *now*, preach the third angel's message *now*, and proclaim the principles of religious liberty *now*.

The men who have the responsibility of deciding for or against that issue should be well enlightened. No darkened mind should be left with that decision. Every person should have all the light that we can bring to them. But merely the question of liberty is not in itself enough. The people must be led to see in Revelation the earnest warning of God against the worship of the beast and his image and the reception of his mark.

The National Sunday Law is also said to be a sign, a signal, that it will be time to leave the large cities. There are three steps brought to view. The first step is leaving the large cities. The second is leaving the smaller ones. And the third is retiring to secluded homes among the mountains. Other references indicate a time when we will be without *any* homes. Do you think this is all going to take more than a few days? Apparently. This won't be a long drawn-out process, however. But we must come to grips with the practical problems that we are going to have to face. It is one thing to stay in the wilderness for two or three days and have a raven feed you, but to actually live there means you would have to find ways to keep warm, cook food, etc. The people who have been used to just flipping a switch and having lights come on and juicers whiz will probably have trouble locating a switch in those cabins and caverns. That doesn't necessarily mean that we are to disregard all the opportunities for convenience now. But if we really believe these events are coming, we must think practically about the problems we'll face.

Some may ask, "Does that mean that people are not to leave the large cities until the Sunday Law is passed?" If we read only one reference on this, perhaps we might conclude that. But there are other statements. We have been advised to:

> Get out of the large cities as fast as possible. *Testimonies for the Church*, Vol. 6, p. 195.

The National Sunday Law is indeed a sign to leave, but it's "the last call." I've been on a railroad train and have heard the man from the dining car come through saying, "First call to dinner." He goes up and down the length of the train. By and by, he comes through and says, "Second call to dinner." Then later, saying, "Last call to dinner." Those who wait after that last call don't get any dinner.

At the present time, we each may be saying, "I'm thinking about getting out." But when the National Sunday Law comes, if we really believe the Spirit of Prophecy and we are still in the large cities, what will we do? Will we *begin* to lay plans, hoping that at some *future* time we can dispose of this and that, then make arrangements, and *then* get out? No. The more we believe it, the more earnestly we will seek now to make that move. So we are to see in that sign the last call of God to get out of the large cities. But we are not to see in that expression to go to sleep now and wait until the Sunday Law passes *before* making plans to get out. No. We should be making plans *now* with that in mind, and we should get out as fast as possible.

I can raise some questions about some great problems that many of our people are going to face when that time comes, but I don't pretend to know all the answers to them. Think of all the divided homes — marriages where one spouse is not a believer, children with ungodly parents, or parents with ungodly children. People need a relationship with God, letting God direct them and help them through personal problems. Or else, like some of the relatives of Lot, they will find themselves clinging to the cities where they feel comfortable. They will be destroyed with those cities.

Let's review for a moment. The National Sunday Law is an outstanding sign of what, regarding our nation? A sign that the cup of iniquity is full, that apostasy is complete, and that the close of probation is very near. What is it a sign of with respect to our large cities? To get out and leave them. Note that, in the National Sunday Law, we have the formation of the image. Read *Revelation* 13:11-17. Who is the lamb-like beast? The United States. What does "like a lamb" mean? When the United States first rose up, there was no pretense to it; the nation came up like a lamb. But, finally, it is going to speak like a dragon. Who is that first beast before him, noted in verse 12? The papacy. The United States will exercise all the power that the papacy used to exercise. What will this nation cause all the world to do? Worship the papacy. It is especially in the honor given to Sunday that the papacy will be honored, because Sunday is particularly the papacy's creation. In fact it is called "the mark of the beast."

In both the Old and the New World, the papacy will receive homage in the honor paid to the Sunday institution, that rests solely upon the authority of the Roman Church. *Great Controversy*, p. 578.

So, in what way will all the world worship the papacy? By honoring the institution of Sunday. The Protestant churches will not give up their denomination affiliations to become members of the Roman church. Rather, in this country, an image — a likeness — to the old Roman union of church and state will be formed, and the papacy will be honored by Sunday-keeping.

As shown in verse 13, the multitudes will be deceived by miracles. But notice that miracles prepare the minds of the people to enter into this great deception and persecution. And having deceived them with these miracles, notice what he does. He says to the people that *they* should make an image to the beast. *Great Controversy* points that out as one of the most definite evidences that it is speaking of the United States, where the power rests with the people. Is some dictator going to seize power in America and make everybody line up with Sunday and the papacy? No, that is not the picture. The people are going to be aroused by miracles and in other ways, and they are going to demand a Sunday Law.

Now, the 15th verse says that something is going to be given to that image. It is *life*, that the image of the beast should both speak and cause as many as would not worship the image of the beast to be killed. Then the eventual result of the persecution brought by the image is a death decree.

What other agencies will be used? Verses 16 and 17 show that the boycott — "that no man might buy or sell, save he that had the mark, or the name of the beast, or the number of his name" — will be used in an attempt to enforce the Sunday Law.

We see then from the Bible that there are two great methods of pressure. One is the threat against life by being killed. The other is the threat against life by economic pressure. In other words, you can take your choice: be killed or starve to death. How would you describe those methods? They are Satan's methods. They have been used in the past, particularly in the Dark Ages. The papacy used them back then; the papacy will again help put those methods in operation. The beast and the image will unite. That is why God warns us to let no man worship the beast or his image, or receive his mark. They are all working together. We've been given a clear statement as to when the image will be formed:

> When the leading churches of the United States, uniting upon such points of doctrine as are held by them in common ...

Do we see that?

> ... shall influence the state to enforce their decrees and to sustain their institutions, then Protestant America will have formed an image of the Roman hierarchy ...

What is the terrible result?

> ... and the infliction of civil penalties upon dissenters will inevitably result. *Great Controversy*, p. 445.

Does the image come before or after persecution? It comes *before*, and it *brings* persecution. And when will Protestant America form the image? When the churches unite on the points of doctrine they hold in common, they influence the state to enforce their decrees. The particular decree is the Sunday Law.

> But in the very act of enforcing a religious duty by secular power, the churches would themselves form an image to the beast; hence the enforcement of Sunday-keeping in the United States would be an enforcement of the worship of the beast and his image. *Ibid.*, p. 448.

So the setting up of the image is concerned with the enforcement of the Sunday Law. In that act, the image is set up; in that act, the leading churches of the United States agree to get the nation to join with them; and over the Sunday question, the image is formed. In the threefold union that brings this about, Rome is not the one who extends the hand. It is Protestantism that will "stretch her hand across the gulf to grasp the hand of the Roman power." Protestantism has to more or less apologize for her independence and revolt, and stretch her hand across. What is accomplished at the time of the National Sunday Law? The threefold union. Protestant influences, papal influences, and the influence of spiritualism join forces to help bring it about. That is indicated in Revelation 13.

Think then of these forces we have to meet — Protestantism in the middle with the papacy on one side and spiritualism on the other. Under the influence of this threefold union, our nation is brought to the place where it "repudiates every principle of its Constitution." What unites Protestantism with spiritualism? Belief in the natural immortality of the soul is a bond of union between them. What bonds Protestantism with Catholicism? Sunday sacredness. Notice that these bonds of union are not in truth but in falsehood. Further deception will result.

> Through the two great errors, the immortality of the soul and Sunday sacredness, Satan will bring the people under his deceptions. While the former lays the foundation of spiritualism, the latter creates a bond of sympathy with Rome. *Great Controversy*, p. 588.

This country will follow in the steps of Rome in trampling on the rights of conscience. The reference adds: "The Protestants of the United States will be foremost in stretching their hands across the gulf to grasp the hand of spiritualism; they will reach over the abyss to clasp hands with the Roman power."

So the two great errors become the two connecting links. As the Sunday Law is passed, it is going to be passed by U.S. legislators, not by a dictator seizing power. It is going to be an actual *legislative* act. The legislators are going to be called upon to take their position, and it will be by pressure.

> To secure popularity and patronage, legislators will yield to the demand for a Sunday Law. *Testimonies for the Church*, Vol. 5, p. 450.

After the Sunday Law is passed, we have seen that there is going to be persecution and eventually a death decree. Previous to that, there will be pressures of various kinds. Notice a few of the expressions on the persecution under the National Sunday Law. From *Great Controversy*, page 604: "Fearful is the issue to which the world is to be brought. The powers of earth, uniting to war against the commandments of God, will decree that 'all, both small and great, rich and poor, free and bond' (Revelation 13:16), shall conform to the customs of the church by the observance of the false sabbath. All who refuse compliance will be visited with civil penalties, and it will finally be declared that they are deserving of death. On the other hand, the law of God enjoining the Creator's rest day demands obedience and threatens wrath against all who transgress its precepts."

The issue doesn't begin with the death decree. *Great Controversy* continues presenting the picture of persecution under the Sunday Law. From page 607: "The power attending the message will only madden those who oppose it. The clergy will put forth almost superhuman efforts to shut away the light lest it should shine upon their flocks. By every means at their command they will endeavor to suppress the discussion of these vital questions. The church appeals to the strong arm of civil power, and, in this work, papists and Protestants unite. As the movement for Sunday enforcement becomes more bold and decided, the law will be invoked against commandment keepers. They will be threatened with fines and imprisonment, and some will be offered positions of influence, and other rewards and advantages, as inducements to renounce their faith. But their steadfast answer is: 'Show us from the word of God our error'... Those who are arraigned before the courts make a strong vindication of the truth, and some who hear them are led to take their stand to keep all the commandments of God."

Our support and stay will be in the Bible. Some of us will have to be taken into court and answer for our faith. But there is still time for people to be influenced. The devil is trying to get everybody that he can to be outside the ark when probation closes. God is trying to get as many as possible in. And both are working against time.

As we are led back to prison, someone — perhaps an attorney, a witness, or a judge — may touch us in the hall and say, "Brother, I have decided to stand with you." Won't that be thrilling? Is that worth getting ready? Certainly. I want to be ready, don't you?

> When the final warning shall be given, it will arrest the attention of these leading men through whom the Lord is now working, and some of them will accept it. *Great Controversy*, p. 610.

It then says that these men will stand with the people of God through the time of trouble. So there will be conversions.

To review, we have been studying the National Sunday Law. It is the great sign to God's people. It is something we will recognize when it happens. Everyone will know when the National Sunday Law is passed. It will be a sign that our nation's apostasy is complete, the cup of iniquity is full, and the angel of mercy is about to take her flight. It is a sign to leave the large cities, preparatory to leaving the smaller ones for retired homes in secluded places among the mountains. It will be not only the bringing in of the mark of the beast, but the setting up of the image. And in that work of setting up the image and bringing in the mark, we will have the combined forces of the Protestants, the papacy, and the spiritualists. Those three will form a corrupt confederacy, a threefold union. Who is it that will actually *pass* this Sunday Law? The legislators who yield to popular demand. And what will create that popular demand are the deceptive, delusive powers working in many ways. Make a careful study of the texts and references on this. We want to know the time of night. We want to know the sequence of events. We want to know the plan of battle so we can stand with Jesus. I have been stressing the importance of knowing the plan of battle, the schemes of the enemy, and God has said it is important. But will all the knowledge in the world in itself make us ready? Oh, no. We must have a personal experience with Jesus. We need both — the knowledge of coming events and a personal experience with our Lord.

Let us open our hearts anew to our blessed Saviour and ask Him to come in and take sin out of our hearts and lives, and fill us with His Holy Spirit so that we can stand when all around us are giving way.

THE LOUD CRY

There are seven phases of the loud cry that we're going to study. The first is the *message* of the loud cry: "Babylon the great is fallen." The fall of Babylon is announced by this loud cry message. Who does the angel say have taken up their abode in Babylon? Devils. Babylon is the habitation of devils.

This picture, speaking prophetically of spiritual Babylon today, is borrowed from the description of the fall of ancient literal Babylon by the ancient River Euphrates. Isaiah and Jeremiah predicted that Babylon would be overthrown and become the habitation of various wild creatures. And that literally happened, didn't it? That also is a picture of the doom of *spiritual* Babylon. She has fallen *spiritually* as old Babylon fell *literally*. She has become the habitation of devils, and the hold of every foul spirit, and a cage of every unclean and hateful bird.

Who are the spirits that live in modern Babylon and finally take over? Satan and his angels. What do we call the belief in and the practice of communication with those spirits? Spiritualism — something that is filling up the churches today. We studied in the previous chapter how Protestantism will stretch its hand across the gulf to spiritualism. For centuries, the Roman church has believed in the appearance of saints. So both Catholicism and Protestantism are filling up with spirits who claim to be the spirits of the dead, but who are really the spirits of devils working miracles. So the second verse is a clear description of the triumph of spiritualism in both Catholicism and Protestantism today. The loud cry message is an exposure, an unmasking, of that. What enables us to declare the truth about the state of the dead? Life only in Christ; there is no natural immortality.

What fatal act of Babylon is brought to view in Revelation 18:3? The union of church and state. What is the event which marks the union of church and state in this country? The National Sunday Law. So the loud cry will not only be an exposure of spiritualism and its rising influence in the churches, but it will also be an exposure of the evils of the union of church and state. The two great errors through which Satan will bring the masses under his control are: Sunday sacredness and the belief in the spirits. In connection with the exposure of the sins of Babylon, the call is given, "Come out of her, my people." What two reasons are given for coming out? Sins and plagues. Sadly enough, people will be perfectly willing to put up with the sins if they could escape the plagues. But there is no way to do that. God, in mercy, sends the warning.

The third angel's message does not cease to sound when the loud cry begins. It is simply that the loud cry angel joins his voice with the third angel. And, of course, the first and second angels are still sounding too. So they are all sounding together. In some texts and references, this is called "the loud cry of the third angel." But this speaks of uniting with the third angel's message. They go on together.

What does "come out" mean? Come out of what? It means come out of the other churches, come out of every church that sins. Babylon is a sinning place, and we must come out of it in order to not partake of her sins. What is sin? The transgression of the law. We must come out of every law-breaking church. God's people will heed that call. All over the world, the faithful ones will be hurried out as the angels hurried Lot and his daughters out of Sodom. That is the message of the loud cry.

Let's study the *time* of the loud cry. Do we have any waymarks that point out the time for it? Yes, from Revelation 18, verses 2 and 3. *Great Controversy*, page 389, tells us that even in 1844 when the second message announcing the fall of Babylon was given, Babylon at that time had not made all nations drink. It says that the fulfillment of this is still future. As the result of rejecting the threefold warning of Revelation 14:6-12:

> The church will have fully reached the condition foretold by the second angel, and the people of God still in Babylon will be called upon to separate from her communion. *Great Controversy*, p. 390.

So there is a final reaching of apostasy which constitutes the signal for the giving of the loud cry. We have already seen what marks the completion of that apostasy — the National Sunday Law. After quoting most of Revelation 18:1-4, *Great Controversy*, page 603, says, "This scripture points forward to a time when the announcement of the fall of Babylon, as made by the second angel of Revelation 14 (verse 8), is to be repeated, with the additional mention of the corruptions which have been entering the various organizations that constitute Babylon, since that message was first given, in the summer of 1844. A terrible condition of the religious world is here described." This condition comes about by rejecting the threefold warning of Revelation 14:6-12. It is after the rejection of those messages that the apostasy is complete, and that is signalized by the National Sunday Law. So the National Sunday Law is the time especially for the giving of the loud cry. This does not mean that nothing of the loud cry can be given *before* that time. In fact, there is a statement that says the time of the loud cry had already begun in the "righteousness by faith" movement of the late 19th century. The Spirit of Prophecy uses the expression that the third angel's message "swells into a loud cry."

What marks the *close* of the loud cry? The close of probation. The loud cry will not sound after probation closes. There will be no need for it, as its work will have been accomplished. Revelation 18:4 states, "And I heard another voice from heaven, saying, Come out of her, my people, that ye be not partakers of her sins, and that ye receive not of her plagues." What is going to fall upon Babylon as the result of rejecting the warning to come out? The plagues. When do they begin? After probation closes. Plagues are going to be poured out upon the world, and God tells the angels to hold them until He can call His people out.

Notice the *power* of the loud cry. What expressions in Revelation 18 indicate that it is a powerful message? Note verse 2: "Having great power; and the earth was lightened with his glory. And he cried mightily with a strong voice, saying, Babylon the great is fallen, is fallen." He has *great power*. The whole earth is lightened with his *glory*. He cries *mightily* with a *strong* voice. These expressions reveal great power and strength.

From where does the power of this message come? *Early Writings*, page 85, tells us: "At the commencement of the time of trouble, we were filled with the Holy Ghost as we went forth and proclaimed the Sabbath more fully.... 'The commencement of that time of trouble,' here mentioned, does not refer to the time when the plagues shall begin to be poured out, but to a short period just before they are poured out, while Christ is in the sanctuary. At that time, while the work of salvation is closing, trouble will be coming on the earth, and the nations will be angry, yet held in check so as not to prevent the work of the third angel. At that time the 'latter rain,' or refreshing from the presence of the Lord, will come, to give power to the loud voice of the third angel, and prepare the saints to stand in the period when the seven last plagues shall be poured out." What gives power to the loud voice of the third angel? The latter rain. One of the great purposes of giving the latter rain is that the saints may have the power to give the loud cry. The loud cry is the *message*. The power to *give* that message comes from the latter rain. The loud cry and the latter rain are linked so closely together that we must refer to both when we study either.

What is the latter rain? The outpouring of the Holy Spirit. Where does it come from? The most holy place of the heavenly sanctuary in connection with the closing work of Jesus at the mercy seat. When does it come? At the beginning of the time of trouble. Some people think of the loud cry as a wonderful time when we are going to soar on eagle's wings, and we're going to be so happy. We are indeed going to see some marvelous things, but we're also going to get into trouble. Some people might think that the time of trouble has already begun. But the troubles we have now are just the little ones. The real time of trouble is ahead.

Now let's look at the *results* of the loud cry. What happens when the loud cry is given? There are several things that are going to happen. First: Mighty miracles will be performed — healing the sick and other signs and wonders. Second: Multitudes will be converted — the ingathering of multitudes of souls into the remnant church. Third: There will be an effect on the people who themselves *give* the warning — the experience of receiving the latter rain and giving the loud cry will completely seal the saints by the close of probation. Nothing will ever shake them.

A few statements on those points from *Early Writings*, page 278: "Mighty miracles were wrought, the sick were healed, and signs and wonders followed the believers. God was in the work, and every saint, fearless of consequences, followed the convictions of his own conscience and united with those who were keeping all the commandments of God; and with power they sounded abroad the third message. I saw that this message will close with power and strength far exceeding the midnight cry."

When we read the descriptions of the midnight cry, we saw how the message swept as a tornado over the country. Thousands of people heard it and accepted it within a few weeks. But this says that the loud cry will have power and strength *far exceeding* the midnight cry.

> Servants of God, endowed with power from on high with their faces lighted up, and shining with holy consecration, went forth to proclaim the message from heaven. *Early Writings*, p. 278.

There is a time to be very cautious and careful, but there is a time to be in a hurry.

> Souls that were scattered all through the religious bodies answered to the call, and the precious were hurried out of the doomed churches, as Lot was hurried out of Sodom before her destruction. *Ibid.*

That will be the time to be in a hurry. At that time we won't be planting seed, expecting to reap it years and years in the future; we will be gathering the results of the sowing of many years in the past.

> The seeds of truth that are being sown by missionary efforts will then spring up and blossom and bear fruit. *Testimonies for the Church*, Vol. 5, p. 82.

One other statement on the ingathering of souls, from *Great Controversy*, page 612: "The seed has been sown, and now it will spring up and bear fruit. The publications distributed by missionary workers have exerted their influence, yet many whose minds were impressed have been prevented from fully comprehending the truth or from yielding obedience. Now the rays of light penetrate everywhere, the truth is seen in its clearness, and the honest children of God sever the bands which have held them." It will be a wonderful time of ingathering of souls — in *large number*. It will accomplish a great work for those who receive it. Those are blessed results.

Point number 5 is the *reaction* to the loud cry. There is going to be a reaction both in the world and in the church. Some people will think the loud cry is dangerous, something that should be resisted. Oh, isn't it sad to think that even some Seventh-day Adventists will brace themselves against the loud cry? Some of those who oppose the loud cry will be those who have been in the work many years. They will claim the fact that their long standing gives them the right to decide whether something is true or false. That comes as a warning to my heart and yours. Like Peter, we need to watch and pray lest we enter into temptation. The fact is that some of God's own professed people will reject the loud cry, condemn it, oppose it, and say that it is false. When the angel of Revelation 18 comes down, they will condemn it. They won't receive it. This doesn't mean that the church is going to pieces; it doesn't mean that this church will be rejected; it doesn't mean that this church will drop out. This church, the Seventh-day Adventist church — the movement that God has been leading — will be led straight through to the pearly gates. But many will be shaken out. Many will leave the ship. They will abandon the movement. Some of these, before they leave the movement, will oppose the loud cry and call it a false light. If we are depending upon someone else to tell us whether something is the work of the Spirit of God, could we be deceived? We need to have such a deep experience that, in humility and earnestness before God, we can find out whether something within the church is of God or whether it isn't.

Now the reaction in *Babylon*. How will those people feel when the popular churches are condemned as being the habitation of devils and the hold of every unclean and hateful bird? What kinds of reactions will that produce when multitudes leave Babylon and join the remnant of God's people? In the chapter "The Final Warning" in *Great Controversy*, we find this: "The power attending the message will only madden those who oppose it. The clergy will put forth almost superhuman efforts to shut away the light lest it should shine upon their flocks. By every means at their command they will endeavor to suppress the discussion of these vital questions. The church appeals to the strong arm of civil power, and, in this work, papists and Protestants unite. As the movement for Sunday enforcement becomes more bold and decided, the law will be invoked against commandment keepers. They will be threatened with fines and imprisonment, and some will be offered positions of influence, and other rewards and advantages, as inducements to renounce their faith. But their steadfast answer is: 'Show us from the word of God our error' — the same plea that was made by Luther under similar circumstances. Those who are arraigned before the courts, make a strong vindication of the truth, and some who hear them are led to take their stand to keep all the commandments of God."

That is true both in the church and in the world. The more power Jesus displayed, the more the religious leaders got angry; finally they determined that they must kill Him.

If you were using one word to describe what the loud cry will bring as far as the reaction from the world and popular churches, what word would you use? Persecution. There will be persecution of all kinds. People will be thrown into prison. Economic pressure will be brought to bear so we cannot buy or sell. One of the things that brings increasing persecution is that there is such power. If God did not turn the power on, the persecution would not amount to a great deal. But when the power is turned on, it is going to awaken latent opposition. The greater the power, the greater the opposition from the other side. That is one reason why we don't have so much persecution now; there's not much power being shown. But when the power is turned on, we are going to see the persecution. So we must be ready for that. That same chapter, "The Final Warning," points out that as God's people get into this experience and meet these terrible reactions from friends and foes, they are going to feel wilted. They are going to feel that if they had only seen what a terrible stir it was going to make, they would have kept still. But they can't keep still. What made them speak? The Spirit of God. Nevertheless, they feel let down and weak. Of course, that is part of God's purpose — to cause them to depend on Him and plead with Him for His help.

Finally, point number 6 — the *glory* of the loud cry. The loud cry is more than a message; it is a *revelation*. It is more than something said; it is a *demonstration* — the demonstration of the life of Jesus. In God's book, glory stands for character. So today, the glory of God is to be revealed. The righteousness of Christ is to be demonstrated through His people.

> The message of Christ's righteousness is to sound from one end of the earth to the other to prepare the way of the Lord. This is the glory of God, which closes the work of the third angel. *Testimonies for the Church*, Vol. 6, p. 19.

The last rays of mercy to be given to the world is a revelation of God's character of love.

> We are to manifest His glory. We are to reveal what the grace of God has done for us. The children of God are to manifest His glory in their own life and character. They are to reveal what the grace of God has done for them. *Christ's Object Lessons*, p. 415.

How is the love of God revealed? In deeds of love. The church revealing the love of God in a practical way is found in Isaiah 58, where the medical missionary ministry is linked with the repairing of the breach and the repairing of the Sabbath. That is to be especially fulfilled in the loud cry. Thankfully, God is not going to send His people out to merely say, "Babylon is fallen and is the habitation of devils, and you had better come out before the plagues fall." Coupled with that earnest warning, there will be the greatest exhibition of practical love in practical ministry that the church has ever given. That is the loud cry in its fullness. As I see it, there will be people with a Bible in one hand and a food basket in the other, or a Bible in one hand and clothes for the poor in the other — telling people and *doing* something for them — perhaps giving them natural treatments for their ailments.

Oh, that the Spirit of God may come upon us and give us such a love for lost souls that we will long to *do* something for them, and long to *say* something to them, and so win their hearts that we can gather them up in our arms and pull them out of Sodom before the fire falls.

MARVELOUS WORKING OF SATAN

S atan is going to work with all power and signs and lying wonders, and with all deceivableness of unrighteousness in them that perish. The reason he is permitted to do this is because people will not receive the love of the truth. They had a chance to receive a love of the truth; and if they had, they would have been saved. But instead, they receive strong delusion that they believe a lie. They will actually believe it when Satan gets through with these wonders.

Everybody in this world is going to believe something, and will believe it with all his heart. Each person is going to be convinced in his own mind. Those who receive the latter rain and enter into the loud cry experience are going to be convinced beyond even the possibility of doubt that they have the truth; they will be correct. But those who receive the strong delusion under the powerful working of Satan will be equally convinced that *they* have the truth; they will *not* be correct.

Today, we have the choice of which road we will take. Whichever our decision, we are going to be fully convinced that we've made the right choice. How important, then, that we learn to recognize the wrong road, that we may flee from it, and recognize the right road, that we may walk in it.

There is a time, then, for the marvelous working of Satan. That doesn't indicate that he doesn't work before, because we all know by experience and observation that he's *been* working and *is* working right *now*. But he's not working now with all power.

We studied that the National Sunday Law is the signal for God to answer from heaven with the proclamation, "Babylon is fallen, is fallen," and "Come out of her, my people." We see that this is also the signal for the marvelous working of Satan. In other words, there will be unusual power from above and unusual power from beneath. God is going to pour out all His power from above in the latter rain. The Holy Spirit will be given without measure. And from beneath, there will be a strong opposition to that — the marvelous working of Satan. He is turned loose to work his mighty miracles. We have little idea what that is going to mean. In this work, we are going to see the uniting of three forces.

> And I saw three unclean spirits like frogs come out of the mouth of the dragon, and out of the mouth of the beast, and out of the mouth of the false prophet. For they are the spirits of devils, working miracles... Revelation 16:13-14.

Who is the dragon? Satan. He worked in the days of Christ and the apostles through pagan Rome, and he is working today through various pagan nations and religions. The beast is what? The papacy. Satan is also working through that. And the false prophet? It's apostate Protestantism.

Notice that there are unclean spirits coming out of the mouth of each one of these divisions of Babylon. Babylon is said to be a great city, and the great city is divided into three parts. The three parts are, of course, paganism, Catholicism, and apostate Protestantism. And what is working in all three of them? The spirits.

What is a mouth for? To speak. Who is speaking through these divisions of Babylon? The spirits. What are these spirits? "They are the spirits of devils, working miracles." Can the devil work miracles? It is surprising how many people think that, if a miracle is actually worked, it must be the Lord who did it. That is how thousands are going to be deceived. And yet, all the while, this text is in the Bible in the plainest language: "They are the spirits of devils working miracles."

The question is answered clearly. It needs no interpretation. The devil can and does work miracles. This shows that he is going to work them through paganism, Catholicism, and through apostate Protestantism. Spiritualism works through all three of those divisions. "They are the spirits of devils, working miracles, which go forth unto the kings of the earth and of the whole world, to gather them to the battle of that great day of God Almighty."

Are we going to see a revival of spiritualism with wonder-working power? Yes, indeed:

Satan will have power to bring before us the appearance of forms purporting to be our relatives or friends now sleeping in Jesus. *Early Writings*, p. 87.

This was written back in the days when spiritualism was just getting started. Only those who believed the Spirit of Prophecy had any idea of the way it would spread and what it would finally do. So, today, only those who believe the Spirit of Prophecy can know the full development that lies in the future.

Notice that this is not talking about deluded people going to a séance in some darkened chamber. This is talking about the experiences the *saints* will have to meet.

It will be made to appear as if these friends were present; the words that they uttered while here, with which we were familiar, will be spoken, and the same tone of voice that they had while living will fall upon the ear. *Ibid.*

Did you ever see or hear anything like that? You will. It isn't limited to meetings where people go to consult the spirits. The saints are going to have to meet these devils claiming to be their dead relatives, and our defense is going to be the Scriptures. We must know the Bible texts on the state of the dead. We must be so convinced that this is true that when we see something that looks just like a loved one and talks just like a loved one, and then weeps when we won't listen, we won't break down. We can look them right in the eye and say, "You are not my father (or mother, husband, wife, brother, sister — whoever they claim to be). You are the devil. And in Jesus' name, I bid you go." And they will have to flee.

A few people in the past have had an experience like that. I heard about one dear soul who had a demon appear to her as her dead relative. But when, in humble trust in the word of God, that spirit was confronted with the truth, he changed into his demon form before the very eyes of this saint, and then vanished.

I think it would be an awful thing to be hugged and kissed by a demon, don't you? I don't want it, no matter who it looks like. I think it would be a terrible thing to let our sympathies go out in the slightest degree to some devil, or to accept the slightest bit of sympathy and love *from* it. But this says that the only way we are going to be able to go through such experiences is to know the word of God.

> The people of God must be prepared to withstand these spirits with the Bible truth that the dead know not anything, and that they who appear to them are the spirits of devils. *Ibid.*

When all the churches around us are welcoming these manifestations and are saying it is the great power of God, we must have faith in His word.

Along with the so-called miracles of spiritualism, we are going to see some mighty manifestations of healing. I suppose if there is any kind of a miracle which human beings long for the most it's to get well and see their loved ones get well. If you have ever had any real pain, you know how nice it is get relief. If you have ever been sick very long, you can understand the temptation to grasp at anyone or anything that claims to heal you, unless you had the foreknowledge that it was from the devil. So we need to know what is coming.

> Through the agency of spiritualism, miracles will be wrought, the sick will be healed, and many undeniable wonders will be performed. *Great Controversy*, p. 588.

But that is not the only way spiritualism operates. Revelation 13:13 tells us that Satan also works with lying wonders, bringing down fire from heaven. So miracles cannot be the test at that time. It is very important to know that.

What will be your reaction when spirits appear before you as the departed dead? Or when miracles are wrought before you? Or when the sick are healed right before your eyes? What are you going to say? If someone you've been giving natural treatments to shows only little or no improvement, and along comes a pagan, worshiper of the beast and his image, and he says, "Let me in. I will show you what God will do to heal that sick person." He claims he doesn't need any fomentations or herbs or charcoal. In desperation, the sick person or his family members lets the "healer" into the sickroom. If, in the name of Jesus "so-called," he performs a "miracle" and the patient gets well, what will you say? That kind of scenario is going to be a lot harder to handle than a visitation from a spirit claiming to be a dead loved one.

> God's people will not find their safety in working miracles, for Satan will counterfeit the miracles that will be wrought. God's tried and tested people will find their power in the sign spoken of in Exodus 31:12-18. *Testimonies for the Church*, Vol. 9, p. 16.

Do you know what that sign is? It is the Sabbath. So no matter how great and mighty the miracles that will be wrought at this time in the healing of the sick, unless those miracles are worked in connection with the true sign and seal of God, we can know that they are the works of the devil. After the National Sunday Law is passed is a special time for these manifestations. Just as the loud cry begins before, and swells into that great burst of power, so the marvelous working of Satan begins before, and swells and reaches its height after the National Sunday Law.

Another area of concern is that of hypnotism. Hypnotism was pointed out as an error and the work of the devil early in the history of this movement. But there has been incredible interest growing on this subject among scientific people. Some years ago, doctors and dentists in this area were sent a brochure promoting a scientific meeting held in Birmingham. All who wished to come could enroll for a series of scientific lectures teaching hypnotism. There were several purposes. It was supposed to help some mental patients. A number of dentists are using it regularly in their work. Instead of giving patients drugs before certain procedures, they hypnotize them instead. Although they may claim that hypnosis is so much better than drugs because there is no *poison* involved, the truth is it's simply poisoning the mind *directly*, without having to go through the blood. Even serious operations are being done without giving the patients any drugs at all, only hypnosis. Think of it, delicate procedures trusted to hypnosis! These are just some of the "miracles" we're reading about. Regarding hypnotism, we are counseled thusly:

> This is the science that Satan teaches. We are to resist everything of the kind. We are not to tamper with mesmerism and hypnotism — the science of the one who lost his first estate and was cast out of the heavenly courts. *Medical Ministry*, p. 110.

Is there a science of hypnotism? Yes. It isn't just some foolishness. It isn't just some sleight of hand or make believe. There is a *science* to it. But it is the science of the devil. The fact that it produces results shouldn't lead us to be interested in it. That applies to everything that is contrary to the word of God and the Spirit of Prophecy. But the only people who won't be deluded and deceived by this marvelous working of Satan are those who would rather be sick but do what's right than be well from doing what's wrong. In other words, the saints will be convicted that it is better to die in the Lord than be healed by the devil. Do you feel that way? I trust so.

God is going to work miracles, but He is not going to work a miracle every time the devil asks for it. When Jesus was here, He healed thousands of people. But when Jesus was called before Herod, the sick people were brought in; and Jesus was told to work a miracle. But He didn't do it. There was a time to work miracles and a time not to. And you and I must have such faith in God that we can kneel down by the bedside of the sick and pray for them and do all we can for them, and then be willing for God to lay them to rest if necessary rather than let them pass under the deceptive workings of some demon-inspired practitioner. I would rather see a loved one laid to rest in Jesus than to see them live under the spell of the great deceiver.

Oh, friends, what a sifting is coming. And one of the things that will sift out multitudes of our dear people is the desire for miracles. They want healing. They want signs and wonders, and they want them so much that they would rather have *them* than the plain, simple truth. This part of the marvelous working of Satan will begin before the outpouring of the latter rain. It will begin before the National Sunday Law does. In fact, it is one of the factors that will help to *bring about* the National Sunday Law. Could it be happening right now? Here is something very interesting:

> Before the final visitation of God's judgments upon the earth there will be among the people of the Lord such a revival of primitive godliness as has not been witnessed since apostolic times. *Great Controversy*, p. 464.

It says the Spirit and power of God will be poured out upon His children. That is the latter rain. Many, both of ministers and people, are coming in from other churches under that mighty outpouring of the Holy Spirit in the latter rain and the loud cry. But take note:

> The enemy of souls desires to hinder this work ... by introducing a counterfeit.... Multitudes will exult that God is working marvelously for them, when the work is that of another spirit. *Ibid.*

It also states that Satan will seek to extend his influence over the Christian world by using a religious guise. Is it true that religion is more popular today in this country than it has ever been? Yes. It is called the "Great Revival of Religion." Under a religious guise, the devil will work. Do you think he will have any altar calls? Do you think he will have people coming down the sawdust trail, supposedly giving their hearts to God? Will the devil be inspiring people to do that kind of thing? Yes, anything, just so he can keep them from going where they will hear the commandments of God and the testimony of Jesus Christ. And the more he can work and the more religious he can seem to be, the less chance there is for deluded souls to break the spell and get out where they might hear the truth of God.

We should be careful not to judge other individuals. God hasn't called us to pass judgment upon the work of this man and that man or some other man. But if we will keep busy with the work that God has given us to do, and have a clear conviction of the message that God has given us to bear, we will not have time for what is going on out in Babylon. It is our protection to be busy about our work.

We may hear others say, "Oh, have you heard what is going on? Here is a great big tent and thousands are coming. The people are being mightily stirred. Hundreds are giving their hearts to God, and many are being healed." Will we have the faith to continue calmly and earnestly about our work of preaching the commandments of God and the faith of Jesus? The rallying cry of this popular revival work is unity in Jesus, declaring that we should forget all about these "unimportant" doctrinal differences that separate us. But you and I know from the book of Revelation that the message of this hour, in which God has promised to put His mighty Spirit, is the message of warning against the mark of the beast. So we can't be silent.

The devil will work mighty miracles in great revivals all through Christendom. And remember, those are to begin even before the time for the greatest workings of Satan. Do you know why the devil launches the false revival before the loud cry comes? He knows that if the churches were in a lackadaisical, sleepy state, and the power of the loud cry message came, all the honest in heart would rise up and get out fast. Seeing that coming, before the time of the mighty working of the loud cry, Satan begins to stir things in Babylon so that the people in those churches will think that they really have something and be satisfied with it, and won't be hungry for the bread of heaven when it comes.

What is going on in the religious world right now is one of the greatest signs of the end that I know of anywhere. It is one of the greatest evidences that God is just about ready to pour out the latter rain and give the loud cry. This work of mighty miracles and false revivals is not going to be confined to Babylon.

> Many will stand in our pulpits with the torch of false prophecy in their hands, kindled from the hellish torch of Satan. *Testimonies to Ministers*, pp. 409-410.

That paragraph had best be left without much comment, but it should not be left without much study. If I were you, I would take that paragraph and get on my knees before God and ask Him to help you be alert. We little dream of the great dangers that are ahead.

> The days of purification of the church are hastening on apace.... The signs reveal that the time is near when the Lord will manifest that His fan is in His hand, and He will thoroughly purge His floor. *Testimonies for the Church*, Vol. 5, p. 79.

God is going to purge His floor when every wind of doctrine is blowing. It takes that to sift His floor.

> The days are fast approaching when there will be great perplexity and confusion.... Every wind of doctrine will be blowing. *Ibid.*, p. 80.

When the wind blows through the thrashing floor, what happens to the chaff? The wind blows it all away and leaves the solid, heavy grain. Do you get the picture? It is not alone out in Babylon that Satan is going to be working in a most wonderful way. Right in God's own temple, scenes will be enacted that we can't now imagine. Every wind of doctrine will be blowing. We catch some of those winds at the present time. But God's church is going to stand firm and true. There is no question about that. The only question is what you and I as *individuals* do.

We see in this lesson that Satan is going to have all kinds of deceptions ready. The devil has one great advantage. Error can have a thousand different forms and disguises, but truth is truth.

Suppose I write down a column of figures and ask you to add them up. How many *right* answers are there? Just one. How many *wrong* answers? All are wrong except one. If you would put all those wrong answers in a hat, along with the one right one, what chance would you have of pulling out the right answer? Do you see the advantage the devil has? He doesn't have to keep to a certain track. We do. He doesn't have to live by certain standards. We do. He doesn't have to confine himself to a certain statement. If some of his agents mix things up that he has told them, it's no harm to him. The more mud thrown in the water, the better.

Oh, how much we need to realize that there is just one answer to each important question. And that will lead us to get our answers from God in the Bible and the Spirit of Prophecy. And then we can stand.

As the final act of deception, Satan will impersonate Christ. The following quotes are from *Great Controversy*, page 624.

> Satan will manifest himself among men as a majestic being of dazzling brightness, resembling the description of the Son of God.

We are told that Satan is the great actor, and he is going to finish his great work of deception by putting on a show.

> He lifts up his hands and pronounces a blessing upon them, as Christ blessed His disciples when He was upon the earth.

Perhaps he will repeat The Golden Rule. And it will sound wonderful as it falls from his well-rehearsed voice.

> His voice is soft and subdued, yet full of melody. In gentle, compassionate tones he presents some of the same gracious, heavenly truths which the Saviour uttered.

Satan will speak a crucial deception:

> In his assumed character of Christ, he claims to have changed the Sabbath to Sunday, and commands all to hallow the day which he has blessed.

Then he will attempt coercion through guilt:

> He declares that those who persist in keeping holy the seventh day are blaspheming his name by refusing to listen to his angels sent to them with light and truth. This is the strong, almost overmastering delusion.

However, page 625 starts with this comforting statement:

> But the people of God will not be misled.

The very elect *won't* be deceived. Do you know why? They have so filled their minds with the word of God and the testimonies of His Spirit, and so filled their hearts with an experience of the Holy Ghost borne of heaven, that they will know the devil for what he is. This is a call not only to deep study, but to earnest prayer. And isn't it encouraging knowing that the people of God will not be misled? Safe in the arms of Jesus, we will be carried through the awful time ahead.

TIME OF TROUBLE — PLAGUES

There shall be a time of trouble, such as never was
since there was a nation even to that same time: and at
that time thy people shall be delivered, every one that
shall be found written in the book. Daniel 12:1.

During the time of trouble that is ahead, how many of the people of God will be martyred? Not one. So, compared with the coming time of trouble, the Dark Ages was far longer and far bloodier. There has been nothing like it in the history of this world. But the world was not in any such trouble as it will be under the coming plagues. Probation will then be closed. The third angel's message will be closed. The loud cry of the third angel will have finished its work. There is no work for the salvation of souls after the close of probation.

> The people of God have accomplished their work. They have received "the latter rain," "the refreshing from the presence of the Lord," and they are prepared for the trying hour before them. *Great Controversy*, p. 613.

So the latter rain comes before the close of probation. It does its work during the time of the loud cry. The people of God will have received the seal. There is no sealing after the close of probation. That will be finished by then.

> All who have proved themselves loyal to the divine precepts have received "the seal of the living God." Then Jesus ceases His intercession in the sanctuary above. He lifts His hands and with a loud voice says, "It is done." *Ibid.*

The atonement will be completed. The number of Christ's subjects will be made up. By that time:

> Every case has been decided for life or death. Christ has made the atonement for His people and blotted out their sins. *Ibid.*

Let's review the different points that cluster around the close of probation. First, the third angel's message will have closed. The loud cry will have been terminated. Mercy will no longer plead. The latter rain will have been received. The seal will be fixed. The people of God will have received the seal. Christ then ceases His intercession. The announcement is made that the unjust and the righteous will ever be in those conditions. Every case decides for life or for death. All of this is true at the time when probation closes and the time of trouble begins. Up to the close of probation, Jesus is in the sanctuary. His work is that of a high priest, or an intercessor. But when probation closes, the righteous must live in the sight of a holy God without an intercessor.

> Now, while our great High Priest is making the atonement for us, we should seek to become perfect in Christ. *Ibid.*, p. 614.

When Jesus came to the final test, He said, "The prince of this world cometh and hath nothing in Me." John 14:30. There was nothing in Him that responded to Satan's temptation.

> This is the condition in which those must be found who shall stand in the time of trouble. *Ibid.*

Early Writings gives us a view of the close of probation and the time of trouble:

> Then I saw that Jesus would not leave the most holy place until every case was decided either for salvation or destruction ... *Early Writings*, p. 36.

That is why He is still there. Aren't you glad that Jesus is going to stay there until every case is settled?

It goes on to say that the wrath of God cannot come until Jesus has finished His work in the most holy place. The first angel says that the hour of His judgment is come. That points to the beginning of the investigative judgment in 1844. But that is preliminary to the pouring out of the awful judgments of God. And this is plainly mentioned in the third angel's message:

> If any man worship the beast and his image, and receive his mark in his forehead, or in his hand, The same shall drink of the wine of the

wrath of God, which is poured out without mixture into the cup of His indignation. Revelation 14:9-10.

If it is without mixture, it is the pure substance. So, "without mixture" means "without mercy." There is nothing to dilute it. Let us see what the pouring out of the wrath of God means:

> I saw another sign in heaven, great and marvelous, seven angels having the seven last plagues; for in them is filled up the wrath of God. Revelation 15:1.

The wrath of God finds its expression in the seven last plagues. These are the plagues that fall during the time of trouble. The number seven is often used in the Scriptures to mean completion, perfection. So, in these seven plagues is filled up the fullness of the wrath of God. And the third angel warns us not to worship the beast or his image, or receive his mark, or else we will receive the seven last plagues, or the wrath of God. When the third angel's message has finished its work, then the plagues will be poured out.

> Then Jesus will step out from between the Father and man, and God will keep silence no longer, but pour out His wrath on those who have rejected His truth. *Early Writings*, p. 36.

That makes it clear that the plagues are not poured out when Jesus is in the most holy place.

> The nations are now getting angry, but when our High Priest has finished His work in the sanctuary, He will stand up, put on the garments of vengeance, and then the seven last plagues will be poured out. *Ibid.*

But as soon as He leaves the sanctuary, the plagues will be poured out.

> I saw that the four angels would hold the four winds until Jesus' work was done in the sanctuary, and then will come the seven last plagues. *Ibid.*

The time for the plagues is when Jesus has left the sanctuary and ceased His intercession. People have little idea of the reign of Christ. Many people have the idea that Christ is going to come down and reign here on this earth, and all the nations are going to gradually submit themselves to Him and become tame. The Bible shows what is going to happen to the kingdoms and nations of this world. In Daniel 2, the kingdom of God pictured as a stone does what to all the nations of earth? It smashes them to pieces and grinds them to powder, and the wind carries them all away. So there isn't going to be a millennial reign in this world in which the nations will finally accept Jesus. As soon as the kingdoms of this world become the kingdoms of our Lord, He starts to pour out His anger upon this earth because the people have all rejected Him, except the little remnant of people who cling to His commandments. Notice a very interesting statement:

> These plagues enraged the wicked against the righteous; they thought that we had brought the judgments of God upon them, and that if they could rid the earth of us, the plagues would then be stayed. *Early Writings*, p. 36.

What happens as a result?

> A decree went forth to slay the saints, which caused them to cry day and night for deliverance. *Ibid.*

The saints are crying day and night during this time. What makes them cry? The death decree. Who passes the death decree? The world. Why do they do it? They are enraged against the righteous. What will make them enraged? The plagues that fall upon them. So does the death decree come before the plagues are poured out, or after they start? It comes after the plagues start. Notice the plagues. What is the first one?

> And the first went, and poured out his vial upon the earth; and there fell a noisome and grievous sore upon the men which had the mark of the beast, and upon them which worshipped his image. Revelation 16:2.

Will the people of God receive that sore? No. They don't have the mark of the beast. They have the seal of God. Those who have His seal, the "mark of deliverance," will not receive the sore, but the wicked that have the "mark of the beast" will.

What is the second plague?

> And the second angel poured out his vial upon the sea; and it became as the blood of a dead man: and every living soul died in the sea. Revelation 16:3.

Can you imagine the harbors? What a world it will be. Notice a statement as to the extent of the plagues:

> These plagues are not universal, or the inhabitants of the earth would be wholly cut off. Yet they will be the most awful scourges that have ever been known to mortals. *Great Controversy*, p. 628.

Now the third:

> And the third angel poured out his vial upon the rivers and fountains of waters; and they became blood. Revelation 16:4.

What is the difference between the second plague and the third plague? In the second plague, the sea becomes blood; in the third plague, the rivers and fountains become blood. Notice the response of an angelic observer:

> They have shed the blood of saints and prophets, and thou hast given them blood to drink; for they are worthy. Revelation 16:5-6.

Looking at that, you would think that the people who had to drink that blood were people who had already slain the people of God. But let's notice this comment:

> By condemning the people of God to death, they have as truly incurred the guilt of their blood as if it had been shed by their hands. *Great Controversy*, p. 628.

Have they killed them? No. Before the close of probation some will be killed. In fact, some have been killed already. Scores of people have been martyred for their faith in various parts of the world. There are martyrs in this generation. But this pouring out of the third plague is because of a death decree that the people have passed, though have not yet carried out. The turning of the drinking water into blood is God's answer to their bold and cruel decision to kill His people. If they are so bloodthirsty, it is fitting that their drinking water is turned into blood. We have seen that the death decree was passed before the third plague, and we have seen that it is plagues plural that are poured out upon the world and enrage the wicked and cause them to pass the death decree. So, after the pouring out of the second plague and before the pouring out of the third plague, the death decree is passed.

What is the fourth plague?

> And the fourth angel poured out his vial upon the sun; and power was given unto him to scorch men with fire. Revelation 16:8.

It is interesting that all through the various religions of the world down through the ages, sun worship has, in one way or another, been a connecting thread with many of them. And we know that in the final conflict, the "Sun-day" stands as the mark of apostasy. God permits the sun to become the instrument of punishment; it will scorch with great heat.

What about the fifth plague?

> And the fifth angel poured out his vial upon the seat of the beast; and his kingdom was full of darkness; and they gnawed their tongues for pain. Revelation 16:10.

So darkness follows the intense heat. Next is the sixth:

> And the sixth angel poured out his vial upon the great river Euphrates; and the water thereof was dried up, that the way of the kings of the east might be prepared. Revelation 16:12.

In the time of the sixth plague, Satan will still seek to rally his forces and consolidate them and gather them to the battle of the great day of God Almighty. The devil is trying to unite the whole world against the government of heaven. To do that, he will use demons working miracles. The devil has never had to work miracles to get nations to fight one another. They have been doing that for generations. Stirring up war is an easy thing for the devil to do. For that, he doesn't have to bring fire down from heaven in the sight of men. But to consolidate his position and confederate all his forces, and unite in one great attack against God by the nations of earth, he is going to bring all his forces to bear — spiritualism, Catholicism, Protestantism, paganism — and sweep them all into one big confederacy to try to wipe out the people of God.

A decree will be issued withdrawing the protection of law from the people of God, because they have steadfastly held to the Sabbath and wouldn't accept Sunday, the mark of apostasy. The withdrawal of protection gives the people liberty, after a certain time, to put the people of God to death. The time between the issuing of the death decree until the movement for its enforcement is called "the time of Jacob's trouble."

> As the Sabbath has become the special point of controversy ... and religious and secular authorities have combined to enforce the observance of the Sunday, the persistent refusal of a small minority to yield to the popular demand will make them objects of universal execration. *Great Controversy*, p. 615.

"Persistent refusal" means that when the National Sunday Law is passed, God's people will herald it as the mark of the beast while the rest of the people herald it as right. America will seal her doom when she passes it. All during the loud cry, God's people shout in trumpet tones, "Babylon is fallen." As a result, some of them will be put in prison. They are all boycotted. And all during the time of the loud cry, that conflict wages back and forth. Then the plagues begin to fall. The wicked will conclude that there is only one thing to do, and that is to rid the earth of these "persistent" people.

> A decree will finally be issued against those who hallow the Sabbath of the fourth commandment, denouncing them as deserving of the severest punishment and giving the people liberty, after a certain time, to put them to death. *Ibid.*, pp. 615-616.

From our current vantage point, it looks as simple as can be that when we see that decree, we will know the hour of our deliverance. Yet when the time actually comes, because of the awful trouble we'll be plunged into, we will not be able to see it. When, after a certain time, people have liberty to put God's people to death, the whole world is going to be turned loose like a mob — like they came after Jesus, and like they went after the Waldenses in the Middle Ages. It is the hour that they have set for execution which becomes the time for deliverance.

> When the protection of human laws shall be withdrawn from those who honor the law of God, there will be, in different lands, a simultaneous movement for their destruction. *Great Controversy*, p. 635.

There will be enough unity among the nations, in spite of jealousies, envies, and quarrels, that under the leadership of Satan they will decide to silence the saints in one night.

> As the time appointed in the decree draws near, the people will conspire to root out the hated sect. It will be determined to strike in one night a decisive blow, which shall utterly silence the voice of dissent and reproof. *Ibid.*

Suppose that the time for execution of this death decree is set for July 1 of a certain year. Because the day legally begins at midnight, when would be the first moment that it could legally be carried out? Midnight on June 30th, because the first moment after midnight would be the beginning of July 1. By that time, the wicked will be so insanely mad that they won't want to wait until daylight; they want to strike at midnight. During this time, the people of God will be earnestly pleading with Him for deliverance. Their point of concern won't be their possible death; it won't be selfish. They sense that the honor of God is at stake. They are pleading that His name shall not be reproached. The saints know that, as midnight strikes, the wicked are ready to wipe them out. Thankfully though, we have this encouraging statement to keep in mind:

> It is now, in the hour of utmost extremity, that the God of Israel will interpose for the deliverance of His chosen. *Ibid.*

THE DELIVERANCE

At the opening of the seventh plague, the death decree is about to be enforced.

> He had power to give life unto the image of the beast, that the image of the beast should both speak, and cause that as many as would not worship the image of the beast should be killed. Revelation 13:15.

As we studied in the last chapter, that death decree is announced after the plagues begin to fall. It is the falling of the plagues that arouses the wrath of the wicked to the point where they are willing not only to persecute as they have done in the past, but finally even to pass a death decree. So the decree is announced to the world sometime after probation closes, when the plagues are falling. However, it is not immediately enforced. The wicked will be at liberty, after a certain time, to kill the people of God. Just how long that will be, we are not told. Let's read again these statements:

> As the time appointed in the decree draws near, the people will conspire to root out the hated sect. It will be determined to strike in one night a decisive blow, which shall utterly silence the voice of dissent and reproof. *Great Controversy*, p. 635.

How the devil would be glad if all the dissenting voices would be silenced. It would seem to him an easy task, since they comprise only a small portion of the earth's population. So it will seem to the political world that it will be a simple matter to get rid of the small group of non-conformists, so the world can be in agreement and have unity. Previous to the close of probation, there will come a great revival of religion, and the whole world will feel that religion is the cure for its problems. We are already in that time. Already the world is turning to religion. It is becoming popular to be religious. There are many things we don't know about the future, but there are many things we *do* know. One of them is that the revival of religion is going to continue and increase.

It was religious leaders that led the crucifixion of Jesus. And it was through religious leaders that the Waldenses, and all those who suffered during the Dark Ages, were put to death. And in the end, it will be through religious leaders, not the atheists, that the people of God will be condemned to death. So religion is not enough. It is *true* religion that counts. Unless we have that, the more religion we have, the worse off we are. Through these great religious leaders and their anger and wrath against the people of God, the death decree will be announced sometime after the plagues begin to fall. During the time of the falling of a number of the plagues, the people of God will be looking forward to that hour when the death decree is to be executed. What will God's people be doing during that time? They will be pleading with God. That period is called "the time of Jacob's trouble."

When Jacob was on his way back to his father's house, his brother, Esau, heard about it and was coming to meet him with armed men, determined to take Jacob's life. The last night before they were to meet, Jacob withdrew himself; and out in the night, alone with God, he wrestled in prayer. There was something bothering him, because he knew he had been a sinner. He was seeking God's help. He was seeking pardon. So it will be in the time of trouble. As the people of God see the wicked around them and hear the plotting of treason, they realize that the wicked are intent on taking their lives. Certainly they'll be praying about that. But the thing they will pray about most earnestly is that they themselves may have the faith to go through the test. Even though the saints will be sealed, and will have received the baptism of the Spirit in the latter rain, and will have worked miracles during the loud cry, yet as they enter the period of most intense pressure, they will review their lives; and their hopes will sink. They will see little good, not much done for God.

Do you ever feel that way? Well, it is a good way to feel. It is the truth. And the men and women you pick out as saints of God fittingly feel that way too. The apostle Paul, one of the greatest saints that the Bible brings to view, said:

> For I know that in me (that is, in my flesh,) dwelleth no good thing. Romans 7:18.

How did Paul accomplish anything good then? It was only what Jesus did through him. Paul had no righteousness of which to boast. As the saints go through the intense ordeal, the fact that they are sure to win does not lessen its intensity. Here's a statement that will give us a little picture:

> They fear that every sin has not been repented of, and that through some fault in themselves they will fail to realize the fulfillment of the Saviour's promise: I "will keep thee from the hour of temptation, which shall come upon all the world." Revelation 3:10. *Great Controversy*, p. 619.

As God's people come up to the last hour, the wicked are surrounding them. Some are in the forests, the woods, the mountains, or even in jail. But the wicked know where they are and are coming after them. As the midnight hour draws near, that D-day, the wicked are ready. They can't even wait until morning light. The people of God are pleading for divine protection. That last hour between 11 and 12 o'clock that night is a most interesting hour to contemplate, for it will be the last time in all eternity that the saints of God will ever agonize about anything. We're told that the angels listen to their prayers with sympathizing tenderness and await word from their Commander to snatch them from peril. But they must wait a little longer; there is a purpose for the delay.

> The very delay, so painful to them, is the best answer to their petitions. *Great Controversy*, p. 630.

So it is with us, here and now — delay is sometimes the best answer to our prayers.

> As they endeavor to wait trustingly for the Lord to work they are led to exercise faith, hope, and patience, which have been too little exercised during their religious experience. *Ibid.*

As the hour draws near, the angels too are near. Around the company of believers, there will be an unseen company of holy angels. Then, around those angels, a company of the wicked, ready to pounce upon the saints. And then around those, a company of evil angels urging on the wicked. Four circles. Before the wicked can reach the people of God, they must first pass the angels of God. But that they will never do. They cannot.

> As these wicked men are just about to rush up and slay the people of God ... suddenly a dense darkness, deeper than the darkness of the night, falls upon the earth. *Ibid.*, p. 636.

Can you picture it?

> Then a rainbow, shining with the glory from the throne of God, spans the heavens and seems to encircle each praying company. The angry multitudes are suddenly arrested. Their mocking cries die away. *Ibid.*

At this time, the people of God hear a voice saying, "Look up." They see Jesus by the Father's throne; they hear Him saying:

> Father, I will that they also, whom Thou hast given Me, be with Me where I am. John 17:24.

It will be a glorious thing to have that kind of answer to our prayers. Thank the Lord. We're told that, in rapid succession, other wonders appear. Right at the midnight hour, the sun appears, shining in its strength. Some, reasoning from what they know of science, say that the earth is going to be turned halfway around. I suppose that would have some interesting effects on the streams and the rest of the earth's topography. I don't know if the earth is going to be turned around 180 degrees or not, but I do know that the sun is going to appear at midnight. Just how God will do that, I don't know. But, we are told in *Great Controversy* that "everything in nature seems turned out of its course."

> The streams cease to flow. Dark, heavy clouds come up and clash against each other. In the midst of the angry heavens is one clear space of indescribable glory, whence comes the voice of God. *Great Controversy*, p. 636.

We are told where that clear space of indescribable glory is:

> The atmosphere parted and rolled back; then we could look up through the open space in Orion, whence came the voice of God. The Holy City will come down through that open space. *Early Writings*, p. 41.

The voice spoken of here is mentioned in Revelation. That is where we get the dates for what we are studying now in their relationship to the plague. It is at the opening of the seventh plague that these things happen.

Read Revelation 16:17-21. This speaks of the seventh plague coming immediately before the appearing of Christ. What adjective is repeated in nearly every one of those verses? The word "great." And it will be great — the greatest earthquake in history. Compared with all the major earthquakes so far, including the ones in Lisbon, San Francisco, and Japan, the coming earthquake will surpass them all. And at the same time will occur the great hail and other destructive forces all at once. We are given a most vivid description of it:

> The mountains shake like a reed in the wind, and ragged rocks are scattered on every side. There is a roar as of a coming tempest. The sea is lashed into fury. *Great Controversy*, p. 637.

Indeed, "everything in nature seems turned out of its course."

> The whole earth heaves and swells like the waves of the sea. Its surface is breaking up. Its very foundations seem to be giving way. Mountain chains are sinking. Inhabited islands disappear. *Ibid.*

Catch the force of the Psalm written for that occasion:

> God is our refuge and strength, a very present help in trouble. Psalm 46:1.

I'm so thankful. Aren't you, friends?

> Therefore will not we fear, though the earth be removed, and though the mountains be carried into the midst of the sea; Though the waters thereof roar and be troubled, though the mountains shake with the swelling thereof. Psalm 46:2-3.

The next great picture given us is the resurrection that is described in Daniel 2. As you come to compare it with other Bible statements, you find that this is the only prophecy dealing with both the righteous and the wicked.

There was a resurrection at the time when Jesus rose from the dead. Who came forth? "Many of the saints," the Bible says. Will there be a resurrection at Christ's second coming? Yes. Who will be raised?

> Blessed and holy is he that hath part in the first resurrection: on such the second death hath no power, but they shall be priests of God and of Christ, and shall reign with Him a thousand years. Revelation 20:6.

Will there be a resurrection at the end of the thousand years? Yes. They that have done evil will be raised to the judgment. But the prior resurrection is one in which both righteous and wicked share.

> And many of them that sleep in the dust of the earth shall awake, some to everlasting life, and some to shame and everlasting contempt. Daniel 12:2.

Not everybody, but there will be many who will be raised at that time. We are told who some of them are:

> All who have died in the faith of the third angel's message come forth from the tomb glorified, to hear God's covenant of peace with those who have kept His law. *Great Controversy*, p. 637.

All the people of God since 1844 who have died in the faith are going to be raised at that time. How thrilled they will be to come forth a short time before Christ's coming, given the privilege of seeing some of the final events in the finishing up of the work in this world. That is a special blessing God gives them in connection with this closing message. Who of the wicked will be raised? Those who pierced Jesus.

> Behold, He cometh with clouds; and every eye shall see Him, and they also which pierced Him: and all kindreds of the earth shall wail because of Him. Even so, Amen. Revelation 1:7.

The only way those who pierced Him could see Him coming is to be raised from their graves. And others who took part in the trial and persecution of Christ, and who at different times opposed God's people, will be raised. So both righteous and wicked will come forth from the grave at that particular time, when the voice of God shouts down from the temple through Orion.

Other wonders are spoken of. There will be fierce lightning and voices and thunders. Then:

> Through a rift in the clouds, there beams a star whose brilliancy is increased fourfold in contrast with the darkness. It speaks hope and joy to the faithful, but severity and wrath to the transgressors of God's law. *Great Controversy*, p. 638.

At that time, Psalm 46 will be sung by the remnant people of God as they look up through that open space in Orion and see the glory of God. While that song is being sung, there appears in the sky God's hand, holding the two tables of stone folded together like a book. As both righteous and wicked watch, the hand opens the tables and there is revealed before the world and the saints the Ten Commandments written by God. The words are so plain that all can read them, in the language that each person can understand. The wicked will realize that the very thing they have been fighting against is the law. Think of what an awakening that will be! Many of the watchers will be people who have been taught by religious leaders that the law is no longer binding and that the Sabbath has been changed. But God in heaven will speak from His temple and bring the law out to show to everybody. The wicked were about ready to kill the very people who have been keeping that law. But God's people stand glorified.

Also at that time, the voice of God will be heard from heaven declaring the day and hour of Christ's coming, and delivering the everlasting covenant to His people. This indicates that this experience is at least a little time before the actual appearing of Jesus. How long before? We are not told. Whether it is measured in hours or days or weeks, we don't know. We know it is a *little* time. But the interesting point is that God tells His people when they can expect the return of Christ. He will declare the day and hour of His coming, and the people of God are glorified at that time.

> Their countenances are lighted up with His glory, and shine as did the face of Moses when he came down from Sinai.... And when the blessing is pronounced on those who have honored God by keeping His Sabbath holy, there is a mighty shout of victory. *Great Controversy*, p. 640.

At that time, all marks of care and weariness will forever be erased. The people of God will not yet be immortal, however. That will be at the coming of Jesus.

> Soon there appears in the east a small black cloud, about half the size of a man's hand. It is the cloud which surrounds the Saviour and which seems in the distance to be shrouded in darkness. *Ibid.*

The people of God know that this is the sign of the coming of the Son of man. They have already been alerted by that voice from the heavens as to when He would appear, so they are watching.

> In solemn silence they gaze upon it as it draws nearer the earth, becoming lighter and more glorious, until it is a great white cloud. *Ibid.*

> And it shall be said in that day, Lo, this is our God; we have waited for Him, and He will save us: this is the LORD; we have waited for Him, we will be glad and rejoice in His salvation. Isaiah 25:9.

Every one of the children of God will be looking when He comes. Won't that be wonderful? That is why Paul says:

> But ye, brethren, are not in darkness, that that day should overtake you as a thief. 1 Thessalonians 5:4.

Jesus is not coming as a thief to the people of God. That puts aside the false teachings concerning the rapture — that Jesus is going to someday snatch His people away. The Bible doesn't teach that. We are going to be looking for Him. We will see Him coming in the east on a cloud. And as it draws nearer to the earth, it will get larger and more glorious until it is a great, white cloud. We'll see Jesus surrounded by the angel band. You might think that the saints, having had this glorious deliverance and having been glorified, would have no cause to fear or to tremble. But we are told that, as Jesus draws nearer to the earth, the angel song is hushed and there will be silence. In each heart will be the cry, "Who shall be able to stand?" We know that Christ is our Friend and Saviour, yet somehow His glory in contrast with the weakness of humanity is such that we'll be silenced. That is fitting. How appropriate then that the saints of God should be in an attitude of awe and godly fear as the glory of divinity is unveiled.

> Then the voice of Jesus is heard, saying, "My grace is sufficient for you." *Great Controversy*, p. 641.

Isn't that so beautiful and tender?

> The faces of the righteous are lighted up, and joy fills every heart. And the angels strike a note higher and sing again as they draw still nearer to the earth. *Ibid.*

Right up to the moment of translation, our hope is in the grace of God. While it is true that we shall stand without a mediator as far as bringing our sins to be confessed, there will never be a day that we will walk this earth but that we will be dependent on the grace, the unmerited favor, of God. So as the cloud comes nearer to the earth and Jesus appears closer, we'll be given a view of the awful terror of the wicked as they try to hide themselves from His glory. They will hide in the dens and caves of the earth. We have vivid descriptions of His coming, and the awful remorse and terror of the wicked. Then of the resurrection:

> Amid the reeling of the earth, the flash of lightning, and the roar of thunder, the voice of the Son of God calls forth the sleeping saints. He looks upon the graves of the righteous, then, raising His hands to heaven, He cries: "Awake, awake, awake, ye that sleep in the dust, and arise!" *Ibid.*, p. 644.

That marvelous description could be penned only by an eye witness of the thrilling scenes connected with the deliverance of God's people and the coming of our Lord. The righteous people are going to come forth from their graves with the same stature as when they lived in this world. And as we see the different generations, it will be evident that those who lived in this last generation have truly been the end of the race. As we realize that through them God has made His crowning demonstration, all the more glory will be given to God. Then we meet in the clouds. "We shall be caught up to meet the Lord in the air." 1 Thessalonians 4:17. As angels "gather together His elect from the four winds, from one end of heaven to the other":

> Little children are borne by holy angels to their mothers' arms. Friends long separated by death are united, nevermore to part, and with songs of gladness ascend together to the City of God. *Ibid.*, p. 645.

It is going to be a wonderful trip. *Early Writings* states that the trip will be seven days. When we think about the distance we have to cover, we will have to move rapidly. But I love to think that, on that seven-day trip, what glorious opportunities there will be for blessed reunions or time to get acquainted. Friendships will be formed then that will continue all through the ceaseless ages. I love to think of the way Elder Luther Warren put it, "My best Friend has made arrangements for me to become personally acquainted with everybody who has ever lived in this world who is worth knowing." I want to be there.

This leads us to the point in our series of these studies where we have scanned rapidly the coming events between now and the coming of the Lord. We shall now go back and study more in detail certain experiences through which the people of God must pass in order to be prepared for this closing time of trouble. We'll study especially the latter rain experience, and what the Holy Spirit will do for the church and for the individuals who experience it, and the crisis that the outpouring of the Holy Spirit will bring about in the church.

We'll also study the preliminary experiences which will bring the latter rain. Everything depends upon that baptism of the Holy Spirit. As we have seen, it is the baptism of the Holy Spirit that enables the saints to go through the time of Jacob's trouble without yielding. Without the baptism of the Holy Spirit in the latter rain before probation closes, the saints would never be able to go through that fiery ordeal. What is it that will prepare the church for that latter rain? Why is its coming delayed? What are the things that must take place in the church and in the individual experience before the latter rain can be poured out? These are some of the things that we will be studying in the next few lessons.

Our heavenly Father, we thank Thee with all our hearts for the hour of deliverance which awaits Thy church. We thank Thee that Thou hast told us in such abundant detail what is coming. Not only that we may know, but that we may get ready. We pray that Thou will so prepare us for the latter rain that the latter rain will prepare us for the time of trouble. We ask it in Jesus' name. Amen.

Seal of God and Mark of the Beast

In the remainder of our studies, we'll be looking at some of the things that have to do with the preparation of the people who will share in the triumph of God in this last battle with Satan. This group of people is brought to view several times in the Bible. Let's notice them first of all in the 7ᵗʰ chapter of Revelation. The angels are holding the winds. We know that those winds represent adverse influences of all kinds — war, strife, earthquakes, and persecution. They represent all the problems that are turned loose in the world during the time of trouble. These winds are held back until a certain work is done — the sealing of God's people. This seal is called the seal of the living God. And notice that the angel who has this seal has great power and authority. He cries to the four angels, saying:

> Hurt not the earth, neither the sea, nor the trees, till we have sealed the servants of our God in their foreheads. Revelation 7:3.

This indicates that the sealing work is done before the close of probation. As soon as the saints are numbered and sealed, the time of trouble begins.

> Then I saw Jesus, who had been ministering before the ark containing the ten commandments, throw down the censer. He raised His hands, and with a loud voice said, "It is done." *Early Writings*, p. 279.

The announcement is made:

> He that is unjust, let him be unjust still: and he which is filthy, let him be filthy still: and he that is righteous, let him be righteous still: and he that is holy, let him be holy still. Revelation 22:11.

So the sealing is completed by the time probation closes.

Now let's look at another view of this sealing work. (In Revelation, it is called the seal; in Ezekiel, it is called a mark.) One being from heaven is commissioned and goes through and puts a mark. He is represented as a man clothed with linen with a writer's inkhorn by his side. The commission given him is very interesting:

> And the LORD said unto him, Go through the midst of the city, through the midst of Jerusalem, and set a mark upon the foreheads of the men that sigh and that cry for all the abominations that be done in the midst thereof. Ezekiel 9:4.

There is a great work of destruction that immediately follows the completion of the sealing. The sealing is in the forehead, and the forehead means the mind. It is interesting that modern science has discovered that some of the most important thinking that you and I do is done in the forebrain.

What exactly is the sealing? First, what it's not: It is not something that can be seen. It is not some visible mark in the forehead. It is deeper than that. It is in the mind. It is a "settling into the truth both intellectually and spiritually." A settling into the truth intellectually would mean to have a knowledge of the truth. How much? All that was vital. Not that we would yet understand every verse in the Bible. We will have eternity to come to that understanding. But the mind would be in harmony intellectually with the truth of God. Whatever God believes about any vital subject is what the sealed person will believe. If God believes that the seventh day is the Sabbath, what about the people who are sealed? They will believe it too, with all their hearts. In fact, they will be settled on that fact for time and eternity. So with every other point of truth.

It takes quite a program of Christian education to prepare people for the sealing. That should be our great ambition and desire, every day, to get the knowledge of the truth which will settle us intellectually in it so that we will believe exactly what God believes. And in our minds, we will believe it just as strong as God believes it. So the sealing is a settling into the truth both intellectually and spiritually. Can a person know something and yet not have it as a part of his character? The devil knows that the seventh day is the Sabbath, but it is not a part of his character. He has expelled that truth from his inner heart, and he wars against it. But for you and me to be settled into the truth spiritually means that we not only know the truth, but we love it and practice it. It is a part of our character. We must not think that the sealing is some abrupt act. Rather, we are in the process of becoming sealed over a period of time, and the close of probation must find that work completed. God's people are to be settled both intellectually and spiritually so that they cannot be moved in the time of trouble. They will be shaken and tested to a degree, but not one of them will fail. Why not? They are sealed. Some of us may have the idea that if we've done all right on the day probation closes, then we're saved for eternity; but if we've slipped up that day, then we're lost for eternity. Neither of those theories is true. The sealing is the culmination of a long experience.

In Ezekiel, the angel knows who to mark, seal — those who are sighing and crying about the abominations that are done in the midst of Jerusalem, which, of course, represents the church. That act, that experience, of sighing and crying indicates their attitude toward sin. Sin makes them feel sorry. I don't know of anything that is more of a thermometer of spiritual experience than that. There are those who do not sin who would if they thought they could get away with it. Why? Because those sins do not make them sorry or unhappy. Though they do not sin, they will not be sealed. Those who are sealed will be those who feel truly sorry about sin — sorry about any sins they have committed and grieved about the sins they see other people committing.

I remember many years ago, when I was just a boy, hearing Elder Luther Warren talking to a group of young people at camp meeting. He asked whether any of them had been weeping and praying because any of their young friends had been going to the moving picture shows. Then he called attention to the fact that some children were crying because some of their young friends were going to the movies, and they weren't allowed to go too. Will that kind of weeping bring the seal? No. And if, as we get older, there is in our hearts the desire and inclination to go after the things of this world, and the only reason we don't is because we think we can't get away with it, we are not ready for the seal. Those who receive the seal are those who sigh and cry for the abominations that are done in the midst of Jerusalem.

You will want to give special study in connection with this lesson to the chapter on the seal of God beginning on page 207 of *Testimonies for the Church*, Volume 5. It gives special emphasis to Ezekiel 9. We'll cover in this lesson just a few of the statements, starting with this one:

> The class who do not feel grieved over their own spiritual declension, nor mourn over the sins of others, will be left without the seal of God. *Testimonies for the Church*, Vol. 5, p. 211.

Any weakness in our own character should cause us to sigh and cry. Any sins in the lives of others should cause us to sigh and cry. If we are heart to heart with Jesus, we will weep over sin as He weeps over sin. Without this, we can never get ready for the seal of God.

There is great danger among us today that we will treat the matter of soul-winning like getting people to join the rotary club or the YMCA. We tend to think that it's merely being nice to people and socializing together that will win them. Far be it from me to suggest that we should not be good neighbors and not be sociable. But there is a heart burden over souls suggested in that text that will never come with just being friendly. We must have a burden for souls, among our own people and out in the world, that is far more than good public relations. We must have an attitude toward sin that leads us to be greatly burdened — to weep before God for the sins of others and for the weakness of our own hearts.

What is the seal of the living God that is put in the minds and hearts of God's people? The Sabbath. God says:

> Moreover also I gave them My Sabbaths, to be a sign between Me and them, that they might know that I am the LORD that sanctify them. Ezekiel 20:12.

God says, in plain language, that His sign is the Sabbath.

Speaking of the time of awakening at the opening of the seventh plague, *Great Controversy* says of those who have rejected the truth and are awakened at that time:

> Too late they see that the Sabbath of the fourth commandment is the seal of the living God. *Great Controversy*, p. 640.

The powers of earth that have consolidated under Satan to oppose the remnant have their mark — the mark of the beast. What is it? It is the change of the Sabbath from the seventh day to the first day. It is that mark which is to be enforced by the two-horned beast. The Sabbath has always been the seal of God, and the observance of Sunday is the mark of the beast. God took the Sabbath for His sign when He made it at creation. That was the sign of His creative power. And when the apostate church changed the Sabbath from Saturday to Sunday, that became their mark of the opposing power. The reception of the seal of God and the reception of the mark of the beast, as pictured in Revelation, has to do with these closing scenes of human history. Just keeping the Sabbath doesn't seal us, does it? No. We read:

> Not all who profess to keep the Sabbath will be sealed. There are many even among those who teach the truth to others who will not receive the seal of God in their foreheads. *Testimonies for the Church*, Vol. 5, p. 213.

Notice in *Great Controversy*, in the chapter called "The Final Warning," that it is talking about the loud cry — the time from the National Sunday Law to the close of probation. That is the special time of sealing and marking. The sealing work has been going on all through this message; but when a person is sealed, he will be sealed completely when the work is over. Bread may be in the oven for a long time, depending on the heat. It is kept there until it is done. So it is with the sealing work. God doesn't want any "half-baked bread." And no one is sealed until the work is completed.

Some statements in *Great Controversy* center our view on the closing conflict between the seal of God and the mark of the beast. On page 604, it states, "Fearful is the issue to which the world is to be brought. The powers of earth, united to war against the commandments of God, will decree that 'all, both small and great, rich and poor, free and bond' (Revelation 13:16), shall conform to the customs of the church by the observance of the false sabbath. All who refuse compliance will be visited with civil penalties, and it will finally be declared that they are deserving of death. On the other hand, the law of God enjoining the Creator's rest day demands obedience and threatens wrath against all who transgress its precepts. With the issue thus clearly brought before him, whoever shall trample upon God's law to obey a human enactment receives the mark of the beast; he accepts the sign of allegiance to the power which he chooses to obey instead of God."

Then on page 605, "The Sabbath will be the great test of loyalty, for it is the point of truth especially controverted.... While the observance of the false sabbath in compliance with the law of the state, contrary to the fourth commandment, will be an avowal of allegiance to a power that is in opposition to God, the keeping of the true Sabbath, in obedience to God's law, is an evidence of loyalty to the Creator. While one class, by accepting the sign of submission to earthly powers, receive the mark of the beast, the other choosing the token of allegiance to divine authority receive the seal of God." Ellen White goes to particular pains to show that those in past ages who have kept Sunday sincerely have not received the mark of the beast. It is only after the world is enlightened to the truth that anyone will receive the mark of the beast. Each person will be able to make an informed decision.

> Then whoever shall transgress the command of God, to obey a precept which has no higher authority than that of Rome, will thereby honor popery above God. *Great Controversy*, p. 449.

Two things bring the time for the mark of the beast: one is Sunday observance enforced by law, the other is a world enlightened concerning the obligation of the true Sabbath. The final burst of glory is called the loud cry. And the opposition from the world will meet that.

> As men then reject the institution which God has declared to be the sign of His authority, and honor in its stead that which Rome has chosen as the token of her supremacy, they will thereby accept the sign of allegiance to Rome — "the mark of the beast." *Ibid.*

We're again reminded that none receive it until all are made aware.

> It is not until the issue is thus plainly set before the people, and they are brought to choose between the commandments of God and the commandments of men, that those who continue in transgression will receive "the mark of the beast." *Ibid.*

So the reception of the mark of the beast is future. Yet, all the while, Sunday is the mark of the beast.

Sunday may be the mark of the beast, but that mark may not yet be irradicably imprinted on people's minds. But like a seal imprinted on a piece of paper, you can try to erase it, type over it, or blot it out with ink, but it still so affects that paper that the only way to get rid of it would be to burn it. That is why God is going to have to burn up the wicked. They are so marked with the character of Satan that there is no redemption for them. That is what the reception of the mark of the beast means. It means that there is no remedy. The character of Satan has been reproduced in humanity. But the converse of that is true with the saints of God. They will have so received the character of God that there is no way for them to change. "He that is righteous, let him be righteous still." They are sealed. How is this done? Notice a most important statement as to what it is that accomplishes this work of sealing in our hearts:

> And grieve not the Holy Spirit of God, whereby ye are sealed unto the day of redemption. Ephesians 4:30.

Some people take this verse and use it to indicate that the seal is the Holy Spirit. That isn't what it says. It doesn't say that the Spirit is the seal. The Spirit is the agency that seals us. If this is true, should we expect a special work of the Spirit just before probation closes? And is that what is foretold? The latter rain falls from heaven upon the people of God and causes them to give the loud cry. The Holy Spirit, along with giving God's people the power to give the loud cry, will do something for them in their own characters. The latter rain does not come to cleanse the people of God. That must be done previous to the latter rain. But the Holy Spirit does come to do something for them. He comes to settle them into the truth, the truth that they have already learned and practiced.

There are many illustrations of this. For instance, in tile-making, there is a point when the tiles are still liquid, and you can decide their color and shape. But there comes a time when you can't decide anymore. The tile is finished. That's the sealing. Likewise, for us, it is very important, up to a certain point, to be fluid so we can be molded. It is just as important, when we get to the right position, to be fixed so that we can't be moved. That is what the sealing work does. It would be too bad if the sealing work was done in us before we were in the right condition. That's why God hasn't allowed this experience to come yet. When the time of the loud cry comes with the experiences that are to take place just before the close of probation, every soul in this world is going to be sealed, settled, one way or the other. He is going to believe either the truth or a lie with all his soul.

There are two things necessary if something is going to be sealed. One is contact with the seal. Unless the document and the seal are brought in contact, could you ever get the seal on it? No. But it takes something besides contact. It takes pressure. The pressure wouldn't do any good unless the paper and the seal have been brought in contact. So there are two prerequisites — contact and pressure. The hand of God reaches down from heaven to put that seal upon the minds, the consciences, the hearts of His people, and presses it upon them with the mighty power of the Holy Spirit. On the other hand, there is a mighty power coming from beneath. We have been told that when the National Sunday Law is passed, then we may know that the time has come for the marvelous working of Satan. What is the purpose of that law? It is to apply pressure from beneath into the minds and consciences of men to seal them in error so they will believe it with all their hearts. They will receive the mark of the beast.

There's another part to this pressure, another force that is going to be applied to the force from beneath. It is the civil power that will make and enforce laws, and also persecute. So the power behind the mark of the beast is the combination of the mighty miracle-working power of the devil, legal enactments, persecution, and the mass pressure of popular opinion.

Do you see what will happen? We are going to be caught in a proverbial vise as we experience pressure from above and pressure from beneath. It makes all the difference in the world which way we turn our foreheads. If we are looking toward heaven, we will receive the seal of the living God and be marked for eternity. If we are looking toward this world and sin, its allurements, follies, and fashions, then step by step we will have so yielded to worldly demands and conformed to worldly customs that it will not be a hard matter to receive the mark of the beast. It is so important to be looking heavenward, to be looking into the most holy place, to be looking at the holy law where the seal is — the Sabbath of the fourth commandment. Oh, that God may impress it deep in our hearts.

> Those who would not receive the mark of the beast and his image when the decree goes forth, must have decision now to say, Nay, we will not regard the institution of the beast. *Early Writings*, p. 67.

If we don't say "No" now, then we won't say it then. For people caught in the vise in the middle, God is going to utilize even the power of the devil to accomplish a sealing work in the hearts of His people. The greater the opposition from the world that we resist, the stronger the character we form.

Joseph developed a strong character in Egypt because he had to resist. We are told that as he was surrounded with those sights and sounds of idolatry, paganism, and lust, he was as one who saw and heard not. He guarded his eyes so he didn't see it. He guarded his ears so he didn't listen to it. God is preparing today some Josephs and Esthers and Marys.

In *Testimonies for the Church*, Volume 5, page 216, a pointed question is asked: "What are you doing, brethren, in the great work of preparation?" Two classes are depicted.

One in the worldly mold:

> Those who are uniting with the world are receiving the worldly mold and preparing for the mark of the beast.

And one in the heavenly mold:

> Those who are distrustful of self, who are humbling themselves before God and purifying their souls by obeying the truth — these are receiving the heavenly mold and preparing for the seal of God in their foreheads. *Testimonies for the Church*, Vol. 5, p. 216.

Obviously, in the latter group is where we want to be.

> When the decree goes forth and the stamp is impressed, their character will remain pure and spotless for eternity. *Ibid.*

Isn't that wonderful, friends? God is getting us into position. He is helping us get our gaze fixed upon Him and Him alone. Like the disciples on the mount of transfiguration — they saw no one except Jesus.

When the contact has been established, then the pressure is going to be applied — that glorious pressure from above, the latter rain, and that hellish pressure from beneath, the marvelous miracles and the persecution. The pressure that is coming is unimaginable.

Thank God that, as the result, we will come out of that experience with characters that will be the wonder and admiration of the universe. And even the devil will be amazed. He will stand viewing us as an incomprehensible mystery. I want to be in that group. Don't you, friends?

If we are going into that tremendous pressure, do you think it might be God's purpose for us to have a little pressure now? Do you have any? Are you willing to meet the pressure? Are you willing to pray through it? Say, "Please help me not to get discouraged, but help me to keep fixing my gaze upon You. Rid me of all my perverted ideas so that, when the seal is impressed, I will receive the one that comes from heaven instead of the one that comes from hell."

Latter Rain — Part 1

Be glad then, ye children of Zion, and rejoice in the LORD
your God: for He hath given you the former rain moderately,
and He will cause to come down for you the rain, the former
rain, and the latter rain in the first month. Joel 2:23.

There are two kinds of rain: the former rain and the latter rain. The
former rain is spoken of as the early rain. These are borrowed from
the agricultural experiences in the land of Palestine. The former rain fell at
the sowing time. Without it, the seed would not germinate. The latter rain
fell just before the harvest, and had to do with filling out the grain and
preparing it for the harvest. The former rain fell in the winter, and the latter
rain fell in the spring. The latter rain ended shortly before the Passover. At
the time of the Passover, the first fruits were presented. Immediately after
that, the harvest was gathered. The essential fact is that the early rain has
to do with the germination of the seed, bringing up the grain from the
earth, and the latter rain ripens it and prepares it for the sickle.

Both the latter rain and the early rain represent the Holy Spirit. It is
poured upon those who desire it and sense their need for it. In the time of
the latter rain, we are to ask for it:

> Ask ye of the LORD rain in the time of the latter rain; so the
> LORD shall make bright clouds, and give them showers of rain, to
> every one grass in the field. Zechariah 10:1.

There are two meanings of the early and latter rain. At Pentecost,
the early rain fell. Today, in this last generation, we have the latter rain.
The former rain began the work of the gospel dispensation. After Jesus
had gone back to heaven, He bestowed that wonderful outpouring of
the Spirit upon the disciples, and the seed that had been sown by Christ
and His disciples was seen to spring up rapidly. There was a wonderful
green pasture as thousands upon thousands of seeds germinated. Thousands upon thousands of souls accepted the message. Thus, the work of

the Christian church was started in a strong way. Just before Jesus comes again, the latter rain will finish the work of the gospel. Right up to the close of probation, that latter rain will do its work.

> The outpouring of the Spirit in the days of the apostles was "the former rain," and glorious was the result. But the latter rain will be more abundant. *Testimonies for the Church*, Vol. 8, p. 21.

After giving us the picture of what was taking place in the early church, we have the statement:

> These scenes are to be repeated, and with greater power. *Christ's Object Lessons*, p. 121.

These references make it clear that the early rain was poured out at Pentecost and that the latter rain comes at the close of the gospel work. Notice also the comparison between the two. In Joel's prophecy, God said He had given the former rain moderately. I suppose if we had seen 3,000 people converted in a day, and a few days later a formerly lame man leaping, and then see 5,000 more converted, we would hardly call that moderate, would we? We would think that was far beyond the highest expectations. The only way it can be called moderate is in comparison with what is ahead. To measure anything, you have to compare it with something else. And compared with the latter rain, the former rain was moderate. Oh, friends, what a marvelous time in which we are living. Think of the wonderful outpouring of the Spirit that is ahead of us. I want to share in it, don't you?

Now let's notice some statements bearing on the great things that are going to happen under the latter rain. *Early Writings*, page 278, has a vivid picture of this experience: "Mighty miracles were wrought, the sick were healed, and signs and wonders followed the believers. God was in the work, and every saint, fearless of consequences, followed the convictions of his own conscience and united with those who were keeping all the commandments of God; and with power they sounded abroad the third message. I saw that this message will close with power and strength far exceeding the midnight cry."

Continuing: "Servants of God, endowed with power from on high with their faces lighted up, and shining with holy consecration, went forth to proclaim the message from heaven. Souls that were scattered all through the religious bodies answered to the call, and the precious were hurried out of the doomed churches, as Lot was hurried out of Sodom before her destruction. God's people were strengthened by the excellent glory which rested upon them in rich abundance and prepared them to endure the hour of temptation."

What immediately follows the latter rain and the loud cry? The time of trouble. That is the time of the great test. God's people will be tested by the Sunday Law, the enforcement of the mark of the beast, and persecution. There will be terrible pressure during that time. Notice the glory which rests upon the people of God during the time of the latter rain and the loud cry. Ellen White says it is impossible to give any idea of what will happen in that glorious time, because it is going to be wonderful.

> It is impossible to give any idea of the experience of the people of God who shall be alive upon the earth when celestial glory and a repetition of the persecutions of the past are blended. *Testimonies for the Church*, Vol. 9, p. 16.

We are going to know some things by experience that we can only dimly foresee, and in some cases have no conception of now. Those disciples who went up with Jesus on the mount of transfiguration had a wonderful experience. As John said, "We beheld His glory." Jesus was transfigured before them; He shone in glory on the mount, and that prepared Him for the experiences of Gethsemane and Calvary. So the people of God will go through this experience of glory during the latter rain and loud cry, preparatory to plunging into those scenes of deepest darkness during the time of Jacob's trouble. Without this, they could not endure. But thank God, the saints are going to receive the outpouring of the Holy Spirit. It will be the greatest outpouring the world has ever witnessed. You and I are candidates for it.

> I saw that God will in a wonderful manner preserve His people through the time of trouble. As Jesus poured out His soul in agony

in the garden, they will earnestly cry and agonize day and night for deliverance. *Testimonies for the Church*, Vol. 1, p. 353.

What will be the powerful result?

The decree will go forth that they must disregard the Sabbath of the fourth commandment, and honor the first day, or lose their lives; but they will not yield. *Ibid.*

Like Jesus, they will be strengthened with power from above; and, like Jesus, they will be sealed. They will be sealed with the seal of the living God during the experience just before the time of trouble. What is the agency that accomplishes the seal? The Holy Spirit. And it takes the fullness of the Holy Spirit to thoroughly accomplish the work of sealing. It binds the saints and prepares them to the point where they will be able to go through the time of trouble without yielding and without failing. I thank God for that.

At the beginning of the Christian dispensation, the early rain was poured out. At the end of it, the latter rain was poured out. But I want to think of it as it relates to the individual. You and I were not there at Pentecost. Is there an early rain for us? Yes, the early rain is to fall on us. It is to do a work in our hearts. That heart work which the Holy Spirit does preparatory to the latter rain is called the former rain. So while the former rain fell at Pentecost to begin the work of the church, the former rain must fall on our hearts to begin the work of grace in our own experience.

From *Testimonies to Ministers*, page 506: "In the East the former rain falls at the sowing time. It is necessary in order that the seed may germinate. Under the influence of the fertilizing showers, the tender shoot springs up. The latter rain, falling near the close of the season, ripens the grain and prepares it for the sickle. The Lord employs these operations of nature to represent the work of the Holy Spirit. As the dew and the rain are given first to cause the seed to germinate, and then to ripen the harvest, so the Holy Spirit is given to carry forward, from one stage to another, the process of spiritual growth. The ripening of the grain represents the completion of the work of God's grace in the soul. By the power of the Holy Spirit the moral image of God is to be perfected in the character. We are to be wholly transformed into the likeness of Christ."

What perfects the individual Christian as well as the church? The Holy Spirit, working in the soul. What gives the grain the start? The early rain. What ripens the grain? The latter rain. What does the early rain do? It begins the work and carries it forward to a certain place.

> The latter rain, ripening earth's harvest, represents the spiritual grace that prepares the church for the coming of the Son of man. *Testimonies to Ministers*, p. 506.

The early rain might fall for years; but without the latter rain, Christ could never come. There are spiritual blessings that people have when they are converted, and when they are getting victories over sin — spiritual experiences that bless their souls. But that alone would never prepare them for the coming of Jesus. That is why this world has continued so long. We should be making earnest intercession for the latter rain. But notice why the latter rain is delayed:

> But unless the former rain has fallen, there will be no life; the green blade will not spring up. Unless the early showers have done their work, the latter rain can bring no seed to perfection. *Ibid.*

Suppose it is nearly time for harvest, and great rain comes. But suppose there is no green grain in the fields. Is that rain going to help? No, it won't. Unless the early rain has fallen at the time of the germination of the seed, there would be no point to a latter rain coming.

Continuing in *Testimonies to Ministers*: "There is to be 'first the blade, then the ear, after that the full corn in the ear.' ... Many have in a great measure failed to receive the former rain. They have not obtained all the benefits that God has thus provided for them. They expect that the lack will be supplied by the latter rain. When the richest abundance of grace shall be bestowed, they intend to open their hearts to receive it. They are making a terrible mistake. The work that God has begun in the human heart in giving His light and knowledge must be continually going forward.... Only those who are living up to the light they have will receive greater light." Can we infer from this that there are degrees in this matter of receiving the Holy Spirit? Some get a little and some get more? Haven't we all had the experience of receiving more at times than we did at others? Then comes a statement that we'll want to ponder. Let us see what is going to happen to people who come up to the time of the latter rain and haven't received the early rain in any measure. Let's see what happens when the latter rain falls:

> Unless we are daily advancing in the exemplification of the active Christian virtues, we shall not recognize the manifestations of the Holy Spirit in the latter rain. It may be falling on hearts all around us, but we shall not discern or receive it. *Ibid.*, p. 507.

Think of it. Two of us may be sitting in the same church side by side. One received the latter rain and the other did not. Wouldn't that be too bad? But that is what will happen unless we are prepared, unless the early rain is doing its work. I want to notice what this expression means: "we shall not recognize the manifestations of the Holy Spirit in the latter rain." Do you suppose that we won't even know anything that is going on? Back at Pentecost, did the people who had not received the Spirit know that something was going on? Yes. If cloven tongues like fire sat upon men, and if they began to speak with other tongues and healed the sick and raised the dead, and thousands of people were converted and joined the church, don't you think that everybody would know that something was happening? They knew something was going on, but they didn't recognize what it was. Failing to attribute it to the Spirit of God, they made other explanations. So don't think that when the latter rain is poured out upon God's people it is going to be so quiet that many won't know anything is happening. I used to think that is what this reference meant. But I have learned from other references that it doesn't mean that at all. It means exactly what it says.

In Last Day Events, page 209, it states: "There is to be in the churches a wonderful manifestation of the power of God, but it will not move upon those who have not humbled themselves before the Lord, and opened the door of the heart by confession and repentance. In the manifestation of that power which lightens the earth with the glory of God, they will see only something which in their blindness they think dangerous, something which will arouse their fears, and they will brace themselves to resist it. Because the Lord does not work according to their ideas and expectations they will oppose the work." They don't recognize it.

Suppose you were blind, and someone with great power opens the door and comes in. You might think it was an enemy, and you might try to push that person out. That is what a great many people are going to do in the church at that time. When the angel of Revelation 18 comes and the latter rain is poured out in fullness upon the church, some "will see only something which in their blindness they think dangerous ... and they will brace themselves to resist it." Is this talking about the Roman Catholics or the Methodists or the Baptists? Is this talking about heathen people? No, it is talking about the people in the remnant church. Why do you think they will brace themselves to resist it? Because it comes with force.

Suppose there is a gentle breeze blowing against a door. Does it take much bracing to hold that door shut? No. But suppose a 90-mile-an-hour wind comes against it. Would it take some powerful bracing to hold it?

When the latter rain falls upon this people, it is going to come with mighty power. It will come like Pentecost, but more so. There will be people in the church who will brace themselves to resist it. Because the Lord does not work according to their expectations and ideals, they will oppose the work.

When the Jewish people were expecting the Messiah, they were expecting Him because it was time. The prophets had indicated it. They studied those prophecies. They went over and over them. They talked about it in the synagogue. There were thousands of people talking about the coming of the Messiah. He came. Did they accept Him? Some did. But many rejected Him. Why? He did not come according to their expectations.

That is why many people today are going to reject the latter rain when it comes. It would be a good thing then for us to study deeply how it is coming, and all that God has revealed on the matter.

How is the latter rain coming? How can we expect it in such a way that we will recognize it when it comes instead of failing to recognize it? It is not enough merely to say, "We are looking for the latter rain. We know the latter rain is coming. It will be glorious. We expect to receive it." The Jewish people expected the Messiah to come just as much as any Seventh-day Adventist expects the latter rain to come. They talked about it perhaps more than we do. They were expecting Him. All their hopes were centered on the coming of the Messiah. When He came, they not only did not receive Him, they rejected Him and crucified Him — the very One for whom they had been praying.

So today, many will be talking about the latter rain; but when it comes, they will reject it. Some who will oppose the latter rain will be people who have been in the work for many years. They will think they know the Spirit of God. It is implied that other people ought to accept their decision as to what is the Spirit of God. They will oppose it and say, "Why shouldn't we know the Spirit of God when we have been in the work so many years?" In other words, "You had better listen to us and not run after a lot of fanaticism." Is there a lot of fanaticism that we need to be careful about now, and will there be even more in the latter rain? Certainly. Fanaticism is wrong and dangerous. But those who oppose the latter rain will mistakenly call it fanaticism, and they will expect other people to take their word for it. Should that be a warning to us, friends?

How are we going to know the Holy Spirit in the latter rain? Here's the key: Before Jesus came, John the Baptist came first. He came to prepare the way. He was like the early rain, and Jesus was like the latter rain, as far as sequence is concerned. What about the people who heard John preach, accepted his message, and did what he said? Were they ready when Jesus came? Yes. What about the people who rejected John's message? Did they get help when Jesus came?

> Those who rejected the testimony of John were not benefitted by the teachings of Jesus. Their opposition to the message that foretold His coming placed them where they could not readily receive the strongest evidence that He was the Messiah. *Early Writings*, p. 259.

Those very men who rejected the testimony of John wouldn't accept Jesus. When Jesus brought out a man who had been dead four days, those people held a council and determined to not only kill Jesus but to kill Lazarus.

We often think that if we only had more power, we could convince people of some things. Don't fool yourself.

If they hear not Moses and the prophets, neither will they be persuaded, though one rose from the dead. Luke 16:31.

If people will not accept the earnest pleas of the Spirit of God in the early rain, do not think that the latter rain is going to cause them to change their minds. If people will not accept the earnest plea to repent and change their lives, if they will not accept what the Bible and the Spirit of Prophecy says, do not think that the power of the latter rain is going to cause them to embrace reform — the very thing they have hated, despised, and ridiculed. That is why, when the latter rain falls upon those who have not conformed their lives by the righteousness of Christ through His full character, they will brace to resist it.

In *Testimonies for the Church*, Volume 1, page 187: "God leads His people on, step by step. He brings them up to different points calculated to manifest what is in the heart. Some endure at one point, but fall off at the next. At every advanced point the heart is tested and tried a little closer. If the professed people of God find their hearts opposed to this straight work, it should convince them that they have a work to do to overcome, if they would not be spewed out of the mouth of the Lord. Said the angel: 'God will bring His work closer and closer to test and prove every one of His people.' Some are willing to receive one point; but when God brings them to another testing point, they shrink from it and stand back, because they find that it strikes directly at some cherished idol. Here they have opportunity to see what is in their hearts that shuts out Jesus.... Individuals are tested and proved a length of time to see if they will sacrifice their idols and heed the counsel of the True Witness." This is the work of the early rain. We come up to a point. We pray and ask God to help us. He gives us the victory, and we accept it. We start making those changes in our lives. But that is not the end. Pretty soon He brings us to another point, and He tests us on it. Will we give that up? We pray to God for the help of His Spirit, and we get the victory. We accept the righteousness of Christ, and go on and take another step.

Note the statement "Some endure at one point, but fall off at the next." The issue that somebody else falls on may not be the point you fall on at all. And the particular order in which these steps come is not the same in every life. So merely because you have met the question of the tithe, or given up tobacco or liquor, or some other test doesn't mean that you are ahead of someone who hasn't. God is conducting an individual school on these matters. Point after point, God is leading His people on.

> Those who come up to every point, and stand every test, and over-come, be the price what it may, have heeded the counsel of the True Witness, and they will receive the latter rain, and thus be fitted for translation. *Testimonies for the Church*, Vol. 1, p. 187.

Who will receive the latter rain? Those who come up to every point and stand every test. The order in which you receive them is for God to decide. But it doesn't make any difference what the order is. Every test must be met before you receive the latter rain. Every necessary change must be made in your life. Never think you can dodge one, or skip one, or go around it. It will stand right between you and the latter rain. Let's take the right steps quickly.

LATTER RAIN — PART 2

Upon whom is the latter rain coming? Who is going to receive the Holy Spirit?

> Repent ye therefore, and be converted, that your sins may be blotted out, when the times of refreshing shall come from the presence of the Lord. And He shall send Jesus Christ, which before was preached unto you. Acts 3:19-20.

But before Jesus comes, there are certain times called the times of refreshing — "the latter rain" — that will come just before the close of probation. At that time of refreshing, the sins will be blotted out. Which comes first, the outpouring of the latter rain or the blotting out of sins? Are the sins blotted out before, during, or after the times of refreshing? Until I find something that exactly answers that, I shall say that the two are associated together. The time is so short. Whether one takes place before the other, or whether they take place together, they are close together.

When two events happen at or near the same time, there may or may not be a connection between them. The two events that Peter is talking about do have a connection. The times of refreshing are associated with the blotting out of sins. The blotting out of sins takes place in the heavenly sanctuary. That is the closing work of Jesus as Mediator. But whose sins will be blotted out? Those who have confessed and forsaken them. The promise is to them that overcometh.

> I saw that none could share the "refreshing" unless they obtain the victory over every besetment, over pride, selfishness, love of the world, and over every wrong word and action. *Early Writings*, p. 71.

Those who receive the refreshing have already obtained the victory. Not that they simply want to obtain it or are merely trying to; they have obtained it. Then they share the refreshing. The only way that everybody could receive the outpouring of the latter rain at the same time would be if they had all by that time received the victory over every besetment. The people who receive the latter rain will not be criticizers or speaking foolish words, for they have already obtained the victory. So, the getting of the victory comes before the latter rain. But sadly, Ellen White saw that:

> Many were neglecting the preparation so needful and were looking to the time of "refreshing" and the "latter rain" to fit them to stand in the day of the Lord and to live in His sight. *Ibid.*

What will result?

> Oh, how many I saw in the time of trouble without a shelter! *Ibid.*

Why?

> They had neglected the needful preparation; therefore they could not receive the refreshing that all must have to fit them to live in the sight of a holy God. *Ibid.*

They look forward to the times of refreshing as the time to prepare them. The only ones who get the refreshing are those who have regarded the needful preparation, which results in their obtaining the victory over everything. Those who wait until the time of refreshing to get a preparation can't acquire it at that time. It won't come that way. What a terrible disappointment and awakening they are going to have as they come up to the time of the plagues and realize that they needed some changes made in their lives. By then, it will be too late. The time to prepare is now. If I neglect the preparation now, and think that the time of refreshing will supply this lack, I am like a boy who goes through his elementary grades and thinks, "Well, I don't need to learn much now. I will get it all in high school." But when the time comes for him to go to high school, he can't enter unless he has already had the preparation. The mere passing of time will never bring him a diploma.

I knew a little boy, about five or six years old, who said he wasn't going to go to school and take all that time and trouble learning to read. He was going to wait until he was ten years old, and then he would know how. But you and I ought to know better than that, shouldn't we? We must prepare.

I want to call attention to two things spoken of in *Early Writings*. One is an experience of agonizing prayer. The other is called the "straight testimony." Beginning on page 269, it states: "I saw some, with strong faith and agonizing cries, pleading with God. Their countenances were pale and marked with deep anxiety, expressive of their internal struggle. Firmness and great earnestness was expressed in their countenances; large drops of perspiration fell from their foreheads." Some people are seeking to enter into that experience. It is your privilege and mine to enter in; and if we have the genuine experience this is talking about, we will not feel as if we are simply walking on air all the time. This is not a picnic. It is a time of agonizing.

Most of what we have studied so far in this series of "coming events" are coming events. But what I am quoting now is going on currently, somewhere. And if you wonder where, I recommend that you pray to God that it shall be where you are. I hesitate to bring out an illustration, for fear of being misunderstood. But there is a catchy little chorus that concerns me: "Every day with Jesus is sweeter than the day before." I'm not suggesting that this song should never be sung, but it is so often sung in such a way as to suggest that life is always moonlight and roses, that all your struggles and troubles are past, and that it gets more like honey with every passing moment. But Jesus, in the wilderness of temptation, had a struggle. Jesus in the Garden of Gethsemane had a struggle. And you and I, if we are ever to obtain the victory, are going to go through a struggle.

Please don't get the wrong impression; there is a place for smiles and joys. But the Christian experience of the present time is not a grand, endless "joy parade." I stress that to encourage you, because a constant "mountain-top experience" is probably not what you're experiencing. Sometimes you have to sing by faith. I do. The experience of the present hour for the people is one, if they are following the map. Sometimes, their faces light up with the marks of God's approval. But, at other times, their faces show a solemn, earnest, anxious look. There are a lot of people who don't want that experience. If they don't have a lot of hip-hip hurray and joy and elation, they are afraid that something is wrong either with them or their religion. And the result is they are ready to throw away religion and say,

"Well, it isn't for me. I can't seem to get what other people get." Or else, they want to get hold of some emotional, exciting religion which will lift them up with a wave of enthusiasm, and keep them there. But if the wave comes down, they become depressed.

I think it is most important that we understand how the Spirit of God is at work today. Again, don't misunderstand. I don't mean that we should force ourselves to be solemn when the Spirit of God causes us to break forth in praise to Him because of some blessing we are receiving. "Now and then their faces would light up with the marks of God's approbation." Let's let them light up, and see the smile of God upon us. When pressed under the darkness that God allows, we can give ourselves to earnest prayer. Let us not think that we are rejected. Let us not feel dejected. I read on:

> Evil angels crowded around, pressing darkness upon them to shut out Jesus from their view, that their eyes might be drawn to the darkness that surrounded them, and thus they be led to distrust God and murmur against Him. *Ibid.*

But where can safety be found?

> Their only safety was in keeping their eyes directed upward. *Ibid.*

Who is up there? Jesus. Where? In the most holy place. What is He doing? He is interceding on our behalf. Looking where He is will give us hope and courage. And while the divine Head of the church prays, the body in connection with Him will join with Him in that intercessory prayer. The purpose of it is to prepare for the blotting out of sins. That is what Jesus' heart is set on — getting sins erased, eradicated, and gone forever. That is what the remnant is praying for. They are not praying that what they did last year shall be forgiven. They are praying that the sins they might do today and tomorrow will never be done, that the very roots of sin will be taken out, that they may stand before the Lamb without spot, blameless. I want that, don't you? What are the evil angels doing? Crowding around, pressing darkness. Do you ever sense them? I do. God pity us. Sometimes they have people to help them — people who criticize, suggest doubts, and undermine confidence. They are helping the devil press darkness upon us. Let's not allow ourselves to be used by him.

Let's seal our lips. And when we have spoken un-Christ-like, let's open our hearts to the Spirit of God.

Sometimes, after I start thinking about something I've said, the Lord reproves me. Sometimes He impresses me that I need to make it right. Does God do that with you? Of course He does. Let us yield to the divine Teacher.

As evil angels send out poisonous atmosphere, the good angels are blowing away the evil atmosphere.

> Angels of God had charge over His people, and as the poisonous atmosphere of evil angels was pressed around these anxious ones, the heavenly angels were continually wafting their wings over them to scatter the thick darkness. *Ibid.*

I want to be where those wings are moving. How about you?

> As the praying ones continued their earnest cries, at times a ray of light from Jesus came to them, to encourage their hearts and light up their countenances. *Ibid.*, p. 270.

Notice the expression "at times." The idea that we can walk in sunlight all the time and never have any clouds or darkness is not implied here. When we experience darkness, however, remember that quote. We are not to let depression overtake us. The saints pray during periods of darkness and depression. Do they feel like it? No. People typically don't feel like praying in the midst of darkness. They would rather wait until they felt like it.

> Some, I saw, did not participate in this work of agonizing and pleading. They seemed indifferent and careless. *Ibid.*

It plainly states that some did not participate. Here is a cross reference in *Testimonies for the Church*, Volume 5, page 209: "The leaven of godliness has not entirely lost its power. At the time when the danger and depression of the church are greatest, the little company who are standing in the light will be sighing and crying for the abominations that are done in the land. But more especially will their prayers arise in behalf of the church because its members are doing after the manner of the world. The earnest prayers of this faithful few will not be in vain."

I am about on the edge of something that is very dangerous. But it is more dangerous to be *ignorant* of it. So here it is. Within the entire church, there is represented a little company who are standing in the light. They are agonizing and praying. They are sighing and crying for the abominations that are done out in the world, but also that the church is following the world. Has that time come? Oh, yes. And the prayers of this faithful few will not be in vain. Why is this dangerous? The danger is that you and I will begin to make mental lists of who is in the light and who isn't. But God never gave us that command.

Suppose we are in a group like Israel, going from Egypt to Canaan. Suppose we say the whole movement is going through, so all I need is to go along with the movement and I will get there. It is true that the whole movement went through back then, and the movement is going through today. But what happened to most of the people who left Egypt? It wasn't merely that physical death overtook them. Again and again, the great majority were in rebellion against God and against the leadership. So today it is dangerous to have the idea that because the movement is going through, that almost everybody in the church is going to go through. The Bible doesn't teach that. The Spirit of Prophecy doesn't teach it.

> To stand in defense of truth and righteousness when the majority forsake us, to fight the battles of the Lord when champions are few — this will be our test. *Testimonies for the Church*, Vol. 5, p. 136.

To see the majority of God's dear church leave this church in the hour of peril is going to be one of the most heart-sickening experiences that we have ever had. It is going to be a terrible tragedy. But the preparation for that is being made right now by the worldly trend that we see all around us. Let us keep in mind that the church is going through. No off-shoot is going to save us. No off-shoot is going to be used by God to call us out. The remnant are those who remain. The false-hearted will be shaken out. From *Early Writings*, page 270: "They were not resisting the darkness around them, and it shut them in like a thick cloud. The angels of God left these and went to the aid of the earnest, praying ones. I saw angels of God hasten to the assistance of all who were struggling with all their power to resist the evil angels and trying to help themselves by calling upon God with perseverance. But His angels left those who made no effort to help themselves, and I lost sight of them."

What must we do unless we want to be shut in? Resist. Think of it. Right in the church, angels leave the indifferent and careless and help the ones who resist the darkness. We are a part of the picture. More angels are coming to our help as we go into the deeper darkness, or else the angels are leaving us and we are left in darkness. That does not mean that these people actually leave the church. They go right on in the church in good and regular standing, but the angels of God have left them. Why? Because they made no effort to resist the darkness. They didn't plead with God for victory over their sins. They didn't unite in earnest, agonizing prayer for victory. The angels of God left them, and the prophet says she lost sight of them. Continuing in *Early Writings*: "Said the angel, 'List ye!' Soon I heard a voice like many musical instruments all sounding in perfect strains, sweet and harmonious. It surpassed any music I had ever heard, seeming to be full of mercy, compassion, and elevating, holy joy. It thrilled through my whole being. Said the angel, 'Look ye!' My attention was then turned to the company I had seen, who were mightily shaken. I was shown those whom I had before seen weeping and praying in agony of spirit. The company of guardian angels around them had been doubled, and they were clothed with an armor from their head to their feet. They moved in exact order like a company of soldiers."

This is the same group. They were the very ones Ellen White had seen weeping and praying in agony of spirit. But now they are singing music, beautiful music, such as she never heard. It isn't heaven; it is the loud cry. It is a wonderful, united chorus of music from the group that had before been weeping in agony of spirit. "They moved in exact order like a company of soldiers." Is the church like that today? No. We wish it were. We pray for it, but it isn't. Will it be? Yes. When? In the loud cry. But before the loud cry can come, there must come this time of preparation of agonizing prayer for victory over sin — sin in our hearts and in the church.

I read on: "Their countenances expressed the severe conflict which they had endured, the agonizing struggle they had passed through. Yet their features, marked with severe internal anguish, now shone with the light and glory of heaven. They had obtained the victory, and it called forth from them the deepest gratitude and holy, sacred joy." That is what the music was about. It was the music of victory. They had gotten it from Jesus Christ in the sanctuary as they united in pleading with Him.

Continuing: "The numbers of this company had lessened. Some had been shaken out and left by the way. The careless and indifferent, who did not join with those who prized victory and salvation enough to perseveringly plead and agonize for it, did not obtain it, and they were left behind in darkness, and their places were immediately filled by others taking hold of the truth and coming into the ranks. Evil angels still pressed around them, but could have no power over them." As the result of this experience, some get the victory and give the loud cry. But there are some who don't. They are shaken out, and their places are filled by others who are coming in. They go out by the thousands and come in by the thousands. Are you prepared for that experience? Many of our dear people are looking forward to when people will come in by the thousands. But very few are prepared for the awful disappointment that will come about as the majority leaves. We are going to see both. We have to have an experience of agonizing prayer that will hold us to God and hold us to the movement in those awful times of crisis.

Reading on: "I heard those clothed with the armor speak forth the truth with great power. It had effect ... the truth alone was exalted to them ... it was dearer and more precious than life. I asked what had made this great change. An angel answered, 'It is the latter rain, the refreshing from the presence of the Lord, the loud cry of the third angel.'" Here are some people who are giving the loud cry because they received the latter rain. But before they got the latter rain, they obtained the victory over sin. How many sins? Every sin. Is it a fanatical thing to believe that anybody in this world is ever going to come to the place where they quit sinning? No, nothing is fanatical that the word of God teaches. God teaches that some people are going to obtain the victory. Let us go in that direction. Let us make up our minds that we are going to keep going in that direction, and never stop until we get there. Let's set our hearts on it.

The same people who give the loud cry with mighty power and sing the song of victory are the ones who before were agonizing and praying, sighing and crying. What were they weeping about? Their own sins, weaknesses, and failures. Then they were weeping about the lowering of standards, the awful apostasy that is all about us.

> The class who do not feel grieved over their own spiritual declension, nor mourn over the sins of others, will be left without the seal of God.... They lament and afflict their souls because pride, avarice, selfishness, and deception of almost every kind are in the church. *Testimonies for the Church*, Vol. 5, pp. 210-211.

They are burdened about conditions in the church; and they are not lulled to sleep with a serene song that says everything will come out all right, that we don't need to be concerned. The frivolous chorus to such a tune might be, "Just keep the Sabbath and pay your tithe, and everything will be just fine."

It is true that God will take care of things. It is true that we should keep the Sabbath. It is true that we should pay our tithe and support the movement. But it is not true that we should be unburdened over worldliness. The reason God is going to do something in His church is in answer to the prayers of the faithful few. If you study the experience of these people, there was no thought in their hearts that they were holier than somebody else. They are not boastful of their own righteousness. They are down on their knees and faces in humility of heart, confessing their sins and the sins of others. If we are not among the faithful few, we had better get there as fast as we can. There is nothing to boast about, but that we may claim a place, however humble, that we may seek a place however small, among those who are crying to God for victory in their own hearts and the lives of others. And let us never be ashamed of it. Let us never be scorned out of it, or ridiculed out of it. Let us never come to the place where we say, "I guess what I had better do is forget all that seeking, and just go along with the crowd. I will still get there." No. It takes a special seeking.

Lastly, again from *Early Writings*, still on page 270: "I asked the meaning of the shaking I had seen and was shown that it would be caused by the straight testimony called forth by the counsel of the True Witness to the Laodiceans. This will have its effect upon the heart of the receiver, and will lead him to exalt the standard and pour forth the straight truth. Some will not bear this straight testimony. They will rise up against it, and this is what will cause a shaking among God's people."

What was the shaking Ellen White had seen? She had seen darkness come, and some resisting it through earnest, agonizing prayer. She saw that some don't engage in that work and that the angels leave them to go to the aid of the earnest, praying ones. She then lost sight of the indifferent ones. There was a separation that went on in the church. Everybody in the church is eventually going to resist something — some resist the darkness around them, others resist the straight testimony.

The church is going through, but it is not going through without a terrible struggle. There is going to come a great shaking. And the shaking is going to be brought about by the straight testimony. Those who resist the darkness, and in agonizing prayer get the victory, will be on one side. And those who do not resist the darkness, will resist the straight testimony and those who bare it. Are we prepared for it?

What is this straight testimony? It is called forth by the counsel of the True Witness to the Laodiceans. We'll study more about that in our next lesson when we study further "the shaking."

THE SHAKING

There is a shaking coming. It is going to shake everything that can be shaken, so that the things that cannot be shaken may remain. Those who go through the shaking and sifting will come out victorious with the seal of God. They will go through the time of Jacob's trouble, and be translated when Jesus comes. So it is very important that we understand what is *meant* by the shaking and sifting, and how to go through it.

Hebrews 12:26-27 says that everything that can be shaken will be shaken, and those that cannot be shaken will remain. Do you know who will remain? The remnant is what remains. Offshoots do not remain; they diverge. Every devil in hell is seeking to shake and sift the church. The interesting thing is that God, too, is interested in shaking and sifting the church. God's purpose in that is not that He wants you and me out of it. But we will either have to be cleaned up or cleaned out. We have our choice. When the church is fully shaken and sifted, then all who remain in Zion will be triumphant, purified, and under the unction and guidance of the Spirit of God.

As we see worldly tendencies in the church, we sometimes become a bit discouraged. But the future is bright with the promise of God. God will *never* forsake His church. There is no question about that. And as the church is shaken and sifted, the pure remnant will remain, and all the others will be sifted out. Notice this from *The Remnant Church*, a wonderful compilation of testimonies showing that the Seventh-day Adventist church is going through to the end. From page 60: "There is no need to doubt, to be fearful that the work will not succeed. God is at the head of the work, and He will set everything in order. If matters need adjusting at the head of the work, God will attend to that and work to right every wrong. Let us have faith that God is going to carry the noble ship which carries the people of God safely into port."

I praise the Lord for that assurance. This ship is going to go straight into the harbor. But there are going to be a lot of people washed overboard. That is not going to affect the ship, but it is going to mean eternal damnation to those who are washed over. There is no other ship that is going through. And in this closing loud cry, everybody will either get on the ship that sails into the harbor, or else they will be left outside forever. Isn't that a solemn thought? We need not question whether or not the ship is going through. It will. Our question should be: Am I going to be *on* the ship as it does? Merely asserting our loyalty to the Seventh-day Adventist faith and doctrine and organization is not going to be enough to take us through.

Peter was certain that he was loyal to Jesus, and that he would stand the test. He was sincere. But what was the matter? He didn't know himself. He wasn't ready. The Lord had been trying to get that dear man ready for three years.

> And the Lord said, Simon, Simon, behold, Satan hath desired to have you, that he may sift you as wheat: But I have prayed for thee, that thy faith fail not: and when thou art converted, strengthen thy brethren. Luke 22:31-32.

The difference between our sifting and the sifting that took place with Peter and the rest of the disciples was that they had another chance. We will not have another chance, because our test ends with the close of probation. Do you see how serious is the test ahead of us? Indeed, the church is going through; but there is going to be a great sifting and shaking. The section titled "Ordeal of the Sifting Time" in *S.D.A. Bible Commentary*, Volume 7, page 911, states: "Satan will work his miracles to deceive; he will set up his power as supreme. The church may appear as about to fall, but it does not fall. It remains, while the sinners in Zion will be sifted out — the chaff separated from the precious wheat. This is a terrible ordeal, but nevertheless it must take place. None but those who have been overcoming by the blood of the Lamb and the word of their testimony will be found with the loyal and true, without spot or stain of sin, without guile in their mouths.... The remnant that purify their souls by obeying the truth gather strength from the trying process, exhibiting the beauty of holiness amid the surrounding apostasy." (*Letter #55*, 1886)

There is going to be a weeding, both among the ministry and the people, resulting in a purified remnant that will receive the baptism of the Holy Spirit and the outpouring of the latter rain.

> The great issue so near at hand [enforcement of Sunday laws] will weed out those whom God has not appointed and He will have a pure, true, sanctified ministry prepared for the latter rain. *Last Day Events*, p. 179.

Oh, it is so important for us to understand that. It saves us from reading a lot of books and papers that come from off-shoots. We don't have to worry that we might be rejecting some light. When we get a Roman Catholic book or a spiritualist book, do we wonder if we might get some light from it? If they speak not according to God's word, it is because there is no light in them. And if anybody is in darkness, it is those who have turned their backs on this movement.

We may look at the people among the Protestant movements that have not rejected the light of this message, and say that God still has a people in Babylon and is going to call them into this message. I am sure that there are honest, deceived souls among the different modern-day delusions. But we should not search for light from their meetings, messages, books, or papers. Where are the sinners when the sifting is complete? They are out. Who is in? The pure remnant.

You will find that the words *shaking* and *sifting* are used somewhat interchangeably in the Spirit of Prophecy. You can see why that would be. In order to sift, you must shake. On the other hand, there is a precise meaning to the term shaking that makes the shaking come before the sifting. The shaking refers to the agitation within the church, and the sifting applies to the resulting separation. Let me use an illustration. Suppose I have a large container filled with a number of fairly large objects like walnuts mixed with a number of little objects like beans. Suppose I start shaking that container. What would happen to the beans? They would go to the bottom. What would happen to the walnuts? They would come to the top. There would be a separation in the sense that the walnuts would be drawn together and the beans would be drawn together.

But if no holes had been opened in that container, where would all the beans be? They would be in the container along with the walnuts. Suppose that, somewhere during the process, I made some holes in the bottom of the container. Suppose the holes were the right size to let the beans through but not the walnuts. I shake some more. What do you see coming out? Beans and more beans. How many? All of them. Will they all come out at once? No. But if I shake it long enough, eventually there would be nothing but walnuts in the container after the beans are all shaken and sifted out.

That is a somewhat crude but accurate illustration of what is ahead of in this church. Of course, the illustration needs a little modification. There are places now where beans can get out if they want to. There are people leaving the church through apostasy. Some give up the Sabbath. Some start using tobacco. Some become discouraged and leave the faith.

Others join off-shoots. Indeed, much of what the off-shoots say about the worldliness in the church is true. But instead of becoming anxious and critical, and trying to upset things and leave the church, why not do what God told us to do — stay on the ship and believe that, in His own time and way, He is going to purge the church. Yes, it is a sad thing that we are losing some now. But ahead of us is a time when we will see even more of that.

> Soon God's people will be tested by fiery trials, and the great proportion of those who now appear to be genuine and true will prove to be base metal. *Testimonies for the Church*, Vol. 5, p. 136.

We must not be afraid of being in the minority:

> To stand in defense of truth and righteousness when the majority forsake us, to fight the battles of the Lord when champions are few — this will be our test. *Ibid.*

The majority will go out, but I want to hasten to add that there is much to encourage us. While it will be a sad thing to see people leave this movement, God is not going to be left without witnesses. He is going to have people who will come in and take the places of those who go out.

Reviewing this from *Early Writings*, page 271: "The numbers of this company had lessened. Some had been shaken out and left by the way. The careless and indifferent, who did not join with those who prized victory and salvation enough to perseveringly plead and agonize for it, did not obtain it, and they were left behind in darkness, and their places were immediately filled by others taking hold of the truth and coming into the ranks." We must never forget that. When the church is purged and purified, God will bring in a multitude from outside to fill up the ranks. The purging will open the way for a great ingathering of souls like those who came in on the day of Pentecost.

Notice this statement: "The Lord will work so that the disaffected ones will be separated from the true and loyal ones. Those who, like Cornelius, will fear God and glorify Him, will take their places. The ranks will not be diminished. Those who are firm and true will close up the vacancies that are made by those who become offended and apostatized." (*Manuscript 97*, 1898) There is a sad picture as far as those going out are concerned. But it will be joyous and glorious to see thousands coming in. Thank God, we can see what is ahead.

We are told in *Testimonies for the Church*, Volume 5, page 81, when this sifting is going to take place, and what will do it: "The time is not far distant when the test will come to every soul. The mark of the beast will be urged upon us. Those who have step by step yielded to worldly demands and conformed to worldly customs will not find it a hard matter to yield to the powers that be, rather than subject themselves to derision, insult, threatened imprisonment, and death. The contest is between the commandments of God and the commandments of men. In this time the gold will be separated from the dross in the church. True godliness will be clearly distinguished from the appearance and tinsel of it. Many a star that we have admired for its brilliancy will then go out in darkness. Chaff like a cloud will be borne away on the wind, even from places where we see only floors of rich wheat."

When is the chaff going out? When the mark of the beast is urged upon us, when persecution comes, when pressure is put on, when all hell is moving and the forces of the devil are let loose on this world, and as the dragon and beast and false prophet unite to persecute the people of God, then the church will be purged, sifted, and purified, and the chaff will be blown away.

There will be heresies. There will be wonder-working signs. The devil is going to have a fan of persecution on one side that is blowing against the church and a fan on the other side pulling people out of the church with attractive heresies and the miracles to go with it. And when there is someone in the church who doesn't know the power of God and the righteousness of Jesus, and he sees some working power, he wonders, "What is the use of my staying in here and having trouble when there is a wonderful working power out there? If I go out there, I can keep my job and buy and sell."

So, the shaking precedes the sifting. What will cause the shaking? The straight testimony. It causes the shaking because some people will not only reject it but rise up against it. These people represent the chaff that will be sifted out.

Who is the True Witness? Jesus. Who are the people who give the straight testimony? Those who receive the counsel of the True Witness to the Laodiceans. They exalt the standard and pour forth the straight truth. Where? In the church.

Another word for shaking is agitating. There are some people in the church who think that agitating is the worst thing that can happen in the church. They feel that there has got to be peace at any price. But there is coming an agitation. That agitation is going on, to some extent, now; and it is going to increase. Nobody can stop it. God is determined to get His church ready for the latter rain. Those who go through the shaking and get the victory over sin, through earnest prayer and crying to God, are those who receive the latter rain.

What produces the sifting? The marvelous working of Satan and strong persecution. What ushers that in? The National Sunday Law. When it comes, then the persecution begins. People will go out. It won't happen all in one day, but the greater the persecution, the more the shaking and sifting of the church.

The church is being shaken by persecution now. Not so much in America, but it will be. This persecution comes because of the power in the church with those who are giving the loud cry. That power of the loud cry comes because of the latter rain. But the latter rain comes only upon those who have the experience of the shaking described in *Early Writings*, pages 269-271, which we studied in previous lessons. Therefore the shaking and agitation must come before the latter rain.

Don't misunderstand. Certainly the shaking and sifting won't stop when the persecution begins. It will wax all the hotter. But it must begin in the church before the latter rain can be poured out. There must come this giving of the straight testimony.

Who calls it? Jesus. It is called forth by the counsel of the True Witness to the Laodiceans. "This will have its effect upon the heart of the receiver, and will lead him to exalt the standard and pour forth the straight truth."

There are three acts that God's people do before the loud cry: (1) They receive the counsel, (2) they exalt the standard, (3) they pour forth the straight truth. Note that they come only in that order. One of the great difficulties in the church today is that too many people are trying to do the third thing when they haven't done the first two. If we pour forth the straight truth when we haven't received the counsel of the True Witness and raise the standard in our own lives, we are bound to fail. But if we will start where God starts, if we will individually study the counsel of the True Witness to the Laodiceans, and receive it in our own hearts and exalt the standard in our own lives, then, and not until then, are we prepared to give the straight testimony.

The people who give the straight testimony won't be looking for the job. Anyone who will read and accept the Laodicean message in his heart will find so much to do in his own heart and life to get right with God and get ready for the latter rain that he will have no disposition to spend his time in accusing others or preaching to others about the sins of the church. People whose great burden is to condemn the church and point out its weaknesses and faults show by that very tendency that they do not have a true sense of the weakness of their own hearts. They need to accept the counsel of the True Witness to the Laodiceans.

God is pleading with each soul in Laodicea, with every soul in His church today. Oh, if each would only open the door and let Him in!

Before the coming of Jesus must come that glorification of God's people. Before the glorification must come the time of Jacob's trouble. Before Jacob's trouble must come the close of probation. Before the close of probation must come the glorious loud cry. Before the loud cry can be given, the power of the latter rain must be received. Before the latter rain can fall upon the church there must be a people who get the victory over sin. In order that the victory over sin may come in the church, the straight testimony must be given. In order that the straight testimony must be given, there must be some people who have received the counsel of the True Witness. Right there is where you and I stand.

Each one of us has in our hands the key that will unlock the door to the future. God has been waiting. Some have received it. But apparently we have never, as a people, *fully* received it. If we had, it would have started the chain reaction that would culminate in the loud cry and the coming of Christ.

LAODICEA

In review, we know that God is seeking to prepare a people without fault, to meet Him at His coming. The translated ones will reflect the image of Jesus fully. Previous to the coming of Jesus, they will go through the time of Jacob's trouble. In order to fit them for that, they are sealed with the seal of the living God. In order to receive that seal, the latter rain is poured upon them previous to the close of probation. All those experiences must come to the church before Jesus comes. There are some experiences that must precede the outpouring of the latter rain. Before the Spirit of God can be received by His people, they must reach the place where they can obtain the victory over every besetment, over pride, selfishness, love of the world, and over every wrong word and action. (See *Early Writings*, page 71.)

It is plainly indicated that, previous to the outpouring of the latter rain, there is an experience coming in the church spoken of as "the shaking." That shaking is pictured as an experience in which some in the church give themselves earnestly to prayer, interceding with God for victory over sin. Also is given a picture of a straight testimony given within the church. As that straight testimony is given, there is a rising up against it, because some will not bear it. This will cause a shaking among God's people. This straight testimony is called forth by the counsel of the True Witness to the Laodiceans. The True Witness is Jesus. Some people receive that counsel which will lead them to agonizing prayer. This will lead them to exalt the standard and to pour forth the straight testimony. This awakens within the church a reaction. This is what causes the shaking. That shaking is followed by the latter rain, the loud cry, and the close of probation. The counsel of the True Witness is in the Laodicean message. When is God going to give that Laodicean message? It has already been given. Then why are we waiting? Apparently it has not been fully received. (See *Early Writings*, page 270.)

We have been in the shaking time for awhile. There has been agitation, but it has never led us to that complete experience of deliverance from the world and sin which would result in the latter rain. And the very fact that the latter rain has not come in its fullness proves that we are still in the shaking, and that the Laodicean message has not fully accomplished its work.

The purpose of the counsel of the True Witness is to develop a people who are fitted for translation.

> Those who come up to every point, and stand every test, and overcome, be the price what it may, have heeded the counsel of the True Witness, and they will receive the latter rain, and thus be fitted for translation. *Testimonies for the Church*, Vol. 1, p. 187.

The counsel of the True Witness is the key to this whole matter. If this counsel is received, it leads the individual who receives it to pray in earnest, agonizing prayer for victory. It leads him to exalt the standard in his own life. It leads him to pour forth the straight truth. And things come in that order. There is no way to reverse that order. We are not to expect to see a pouring forth of the straight testimony in its fullness until there are those who have had victory in their own lives through agonizing prayer.

So, at the present time, it is fitting to keep quiet about some things. There is a certain amount of work that can be done today in trying to hold the lines against worldliness. But there are hundreds and thousands of things that there is very little that we can at present do about except pray, plead, sigh, and cry. If we will do those things, it will lead us to the place of seeing our own condition, our own personal weakness and neediness. It will lead us to the place where instead of feeling critical of others we will say, "Oh God, I feel so unworthy and so needy and bad that I am unable to cope with things." And as we cry to God, He will give the strength and victory in our own lives. Then there will finally come the commission. We cannot select and appoint ourselves. If we run without the divine commission, we will be disappointed in the end. But sometime, God is going to send to His people a message of reproof and rebuke that will shake, stir, and sift.

Read Revelation 3:14-22. It is the message to the Laodiceans. The messages to the seven churches that we find in Revelation chapters 2 and 3 were directed first of all to seven literal churches in Asia Minor. Their names are given in Revelation 1:11 — Ephesus, Smyrna, Pergamos, Thyatira, Sardis, Philadelphia, and Laodicea. There was an actual church called Laodicea. And the message was first of all to them back when John was on the isle of Patmos. But while that is true historically, it is also seen fit to picture those seven churches as successive states of the church down through the ages. And the Laodicean church is the seventh one on the list. Let us draw insight from the Spirit of Prophecy about this. First, the application that applies to us today:

> The Laodicean message applies to the people of God who profess to believe present truth. The greater part are lukewarm professors, having a name but no zeal. *Testimonies for the Church*, Vol. 4, p. 87.

In the message to the Laodiceans, there is nothing said in the way of criticizing their doctrines. In some of the messages to these churches, you will find suggestions that they were not teaching the right things, but not in the case of the Laodiceans. The Laodiceans have truth, but their problem is in another direction. It is in their experience.

> The message to the church of the Laodiceans is a startling denunciation, and is applicable to the people of God at the present time. *Testimonies for the Church*, Vol. 3, p. 252.

Who is speaking the message? Jesus. "These things saith the Amen, the faithful and true witness, the beginning of the creation of God." It is through Him and by Him that all the work of creation is done. So, having established the identity of the One who is speaking, He begins His message, "I know thy works." You will find this repeated down through the messages to the other churches. In many cases when He says, "I know thy works," it is some message of appreciation and encouragement. But in the message to the Laodiceans, there is not one word of approval. That should come to us with great force. He is rebuking us.

"I know thy works, that thou art neither cold nor hot." In reference to each other, cold and hot are opposites. The difficulty with the Laodiceans is that they are neither cold nor hot.

> The only hope for the Laodiceans is a clear view of their standing before God, a knowledge of the nature of their disease. They are neither cold nor hot; they occupy a neutral position, and at the same time flatter themselves that they are in need of nothing. *Testimonies for the Church*, Vol. 4, p. 87.

This is what God says. He is analyzing us. He says that our position as a people is in being in the middle. We are not cold like the wicked world, and we are not hot and on fire like the apostolic church. He doesn't charge us with going to horse races and gambling and drinking and murder. He doesn't charge us with false doctrines of Sunday keeping, eternal torment, and spiritualism. But He says that our difficulty is that we are lukewarm, neutral, Laodicean. If a person is cold, he usually wishes for warmth. But a lukewarm condition is quite satisfied.

> The True Witness hates this lukewarmness. He loathes the indifference of this class of persons. Said He: "I would that thou wert cold or hot." *Ibid.*

God would rather have people be unconverted than in a Laodicean condition. He would be better pleased if lukewarm professors had never named His name. That is the Laodicean message, a startling rebuke. "I would thou wert cold or hot. So then because thou art lukewarm, and neither cold nor hot, I will spue thee out of My mouth." The spewing out of the mouth indicates that Jesus will finally reject the individual who continues being Laodicean. It doesn't mean that God is going to reject this denomination. Think nothing of the kind. We have already proved that this message, this denomination, this organization is going to go through to the kingdom. But this shaking we are studying, with the sifting that follows it, is going to purge out of the church those who remain lukewarm. And the purpose of the message to the Laodiceans is to arouse God's people to shake off this lethargy, to get rid of this lukewarmness, and get into the experience where the latter rain can fall. But to those who persist in rejecting the Laodicean message, the only result is to be spewed out of Christ's mouth, rejected, and cast aside.

Ellen White saw in the vision of the shaking that some persons were lost sight of. The numbers of the company lessened, but eventually others came in from the world to take their place. Now let's see what Laodicea says. "Because thou sayest, I am rich, and increased with goods, and have need of nothing; and knowest not that thou art wretched, and miserable, and poor, and blind, and naked: I counsel thee to buy of Me gold tried in the fire, that thou mayest be rich; and white raiment, that thou mayest be clothed, and that the shame of thy nakedness do not appear; and anoint thine eyes with eyesalve, that thou mayest see."

I was interested in a statement on this matter of "rich." One of the things that makes Laodicea feel rich is because there is so much material wealth. They are like the Jews who looked at that beautiful temple adorned with gold and all kinds of precious material and took pride in it, allowing themselves to suppose that their wealth measured their acceptance with God and their development in religious matters. Nothing could be further from the truth.

Testimonies for the Church, Volume 1, page 141, states: "The Lord has shown me in vision some things concerning the church in its present lukewarm state.... The danger of God's people for a few years past has been the love of the world. Out of this have sprung the sins of selfishness and covetousness. The more they get of this world, the more they set their affections on it; and still they reach out for more. Said the angel: 'It is easier for a camel to go through a needle's eye, than for a rich man to enter into the kingdom of God.' Yet many who profess to believe that we are having the last note of warning to the world, are striving with all their energies to place themselves in a position where it is easier for a camel to go through a needle's eye than for them to enter the kingdom." They are trying to get what? Rich. Material wealth. And having such affluence, as many in the church do at the present time, it is easy for them to conclude that God is blessing, and that the material prosperity is evidence of spiritual prosperity. That is not necessarily true. We say we are rich; but God says we are wretched, miserable, poor, blind, and naked.

Now comes the counsel. And the reason He is giving us this counsel is because we do not sense our need of these things. He is counseling us to buy things that we do not fully appreciate our need of. So we will have to accept His counsel just because He says it. And I pray that somehow this will become a personal matter to us all, and that we shall personally receive the counsel of the True Witness. There are three things He wants us to buy — gold, white raiment, and eyesalve. The gold:

> They will feel the necessity of buying gold, which is pure faith and love. *Testimonies for the Church*, Vol. 3, p. 254.

> Faith and love are the true riches, the pure gold which the True Witness counsels the lukewarm to buy. *Testimonies for the Church*, Vol. 4, p. 88.

> So many times faith and love are linked together. Then the white raiment is spoken of as character, the righteousness of Christ: ... White raiment, which is a spotless character made pure in the blood of their dear Redeemer. *Testimonies for the Church*, Vol. 3, p. 254.

In the parable of the marriage of the king's son, the king furnished the wedding garment to each guest. He came in to see how they were clothed. There was one man who didn't have on the wedding garment. He was cast out. Our only hope of going through the investigative judgment is to have on white raiment, a spotless character, without blemish or fault of any kind. Then the eyesalve:

> And eyesalve, which is the grace of God and which will give clear discernment of spiritual things and detect sin. *Ibid.*

I was interested in a statement which says that God has given eyes to His church, but there are some who would like to put out the eyes of the church. They don't want their sins to be seen. In *Testimonies for the Church*, Volume 4, page 88, it states: "The eyesalve is that wisdom and grace which enables us to discern between the evil and the good, and to detect sin under any guise. God has given His church eyes which He requires them to anoint with wisdom, that they may see clearly; but many would put out the eyes of the church if they could; for they would not have their deeds come to the light, lest they should be reproved. The divine eyesalve will impart clearness to the understanding." It is amazing to me how utterly blind we can be. But a person whose eyes have been anointed with this eyesalve will be able to see — to see straight through the designs of the enemy and to discern right from wrong.

With thousands of people today, the main question is: "Who advocates it?" If someone they have confidence in recommends it, they are ready to swallow it. But God is looking for people whose eyes have been anointed with eyesalve, people who can see for themselves what is right and what is wrong. Not that we should avoid counsel. We should appreciate counsel. But the purpose of counsel should be to enable us to see for ourselves the harm in a wrong course, or the righteousness in a proper course.

In ancient times, a prophet was called a "seer." The Spirit of Prophecy has been well spoken of as "the eyes of the church." However:

> Many are going directly contrary to the light which God has given to His people, because they do not read the books which contain the light and knowledge in cautions, reproofs, and warnings. *Testimonies for the Church*, Vol. 5, p. 681.

If you and I will read what the prophet has written, we can have eyes that see. Many years ago, before any of us were born, the Spirit of Prophecy counseled that the place for our children until they were eight or ten years of age was outside of the schoolroom. The Lord told us that the parents should be the teacher, and nature was to be the lesson book. How many of our people follow that? I'm not trying to condemn anyone. I am trying to get us to realize how little we look through the eyes of the Spirit of Prophecy. We tend to look through the eyes of custom and habit around us. We look to our own experience and to the advice and opinions of people in the world and in the church. Isn't that a sad truth?

God is looking for people who will look at every subject through the eyes of the Spirit of Prophecy, who will accept the grace that will enable us to detect sin. In health reform, dress reform, educational reform, the books we read, the music we sing and play, the work we do, we shall look at these as God looks at them. We need the anointing eyesalve to see, in their true light, the things that we have looked upon as good and desirable — to see that they are really wretched and miserable.

There are many people today who are "blind" — they "can't see" the good in health reform, dress reform, and educational reform. The question we need to ask ourselves is, "Where are we blind?" Very few of us are blind on everything, but our difficulty is that we have "blind spots." And one of our greatest difficulties is being able to see ourselves. Oh, that God will give us the spiritual grace of the eyesalve so that we have the necessary discernment. This is our only hope.

Imagine a blind man going in to meet a king. Someone stops him and says, "Where are you going?" He answers, "I am going to meet the king." The seeing man replies, "Don't you think you ought to get better dressed first?" The blind man responds, "I dressed before I came." But low and behold, he is in rags that are in tatters and filthy. What does he need? He needs eyesalve. He needs to have his eyes opened. Then he can look at himself and think, "My, was I really going in there to meet the king in this condition? What was the matter with me? I must have been blind." The eyesalve will enable us to see. Then we will want the white raiment, the righteousness of Christ. We will plead for it.

Now I come to something that, to me, is very important in this study — to understand what Jesus meant in the word "buy" when He said, "I counsel to buy of Me gold tried in the fire." We very seldom hear the blessings of salvation presented as something to be bought. We usually hear them presented as something free. And they are free as far as *money* is concerned. Then why does Jesus say "buy"?

From *Testimonies for the Church*, Volume 1, page 142: "Heed the counsel of the True Witness. Buy gold tried in the fire, that thou mayest be rich, white raiment that thou mayest be clothed, and eyesalve that thou mayest see. Make some effort. These precious treasures will not drop upon us without some exertion on our part. We must buy — 'be zealous and repent' of our lukewarm state. We must be awake to see our wrongs, to search for our sins, and to zealously repent of them." "Buying," in this sense, indicates that we must make some effort. We must go after it. We can't just sit back and say, "I hope it will happen sometime." We must buy, not with money, but with our effort — a supreme endeavor — to receive these wonderful blessings.

We have already seen that faith and love is the gold. We are told that those are the things that are most lacking among God's people today. One of the greatest examples of love in the Bible is the experience of Moses. I want you to see the experience of this man of whom God thought so highly. Moses had been called up into Mount Sinai, and given the directions for making the sanctuary. To him had been delivered the two tables of stone. While Moses was up there in the mount, the congregation went into apostasy. They persuaded Aaron to lead them in making a golden calf. God told Moses what had happened. Even before Moses got into the camp, he saw what was going on. His soul rose up in indignation against that terrible apostasy, and he threw down those tables of stone and broke them. That was not a sin. It was an expression of God's own attitude on the matter. God too was indignant at that terrible apostasy, and Moses was heart to heart with God.

After Moses had rebuked the people and Aaron, he said: "Ye have sinned a great sin: and now I will go up unto the LORD; peradventure I shall make an atonement for your sin. And Moses returned unto the LORD, and said, Oh, this people have sinned a great sin, and have made them gods of gold. Yet now, if Thou wilt forgive their sin—;and if not, blot me, I pray Thee, out of Thy book which Thou hast written." (Exodus 32:30-32) Moses was not trying to get them *punished*. He was trying to get them pardoned. Why? Because he *loved* them. This is one of the greatest examples that I know of love, outside of Jesus Himself. Moses loved Israel so much that he was willing to die and be blotted out of existence rather than see them lost. He couldn't bear the thought of Israel being set aside. God had offered to Moses the opportunity to have his family be the chosen people, and to have Israel blotted out. God could safely offer that to Moses because He knew that he would turn it down.

There are some people today who think that God has told them that the church is rejected, and that He is going to use them in some off-shoot. They don't have the spirit of Moses. Moses began to plead with God. He began to reason with Him, saying that if the people who are called by God's name are destroyed, and all the heathen hear of it, what would that do to His great name? The people upon whom God will put His Spirit today will have that attitude. Instead of being interested in an off-shoot where they can make a great name, or help someone else make a great name, they will be zealous for the name of God.

God led this movement out of Babylon as He led Israel out of Egypt. He has, in the prophecies, indicated that this is the time for the last movement. We have, since 1844, been heralding that last message. It would bring great reproach to the name of God if this movement had to be rejected, and some other movement was started up. And those who love the name of God cannot bear any such thought. Those who really feel heart to heart with Jesus in this love for God and His people, and love for the truth, will be pleading as Moses did and ask the Lord to do whatever it takes to save the people — to save this church. That is the pure gold that we are to buy. It is this love which cannot let go. But, in it, there is no compromise with sin. The same Moses, who was up there pleading with God that Israel be not rejected, was the one who threw down the tables of stone, rebuked Aaron, and demanded that there be a reformation.

Love and discipline are united. They are not opposed to each other. The Heavenly Merchantman is knocking on doors in modern-day Laodicea. He has something that you need to buy: gold, pure gold — true faith and pure love. He counsels us to buy it.

Do we have the kind of love that Moses had? If we don't, we ought to be seeking it with all the earnestness and intensity that God can give us. We should ask for a love so great that we would rather die than see God's church blotted out and destroyed. That is the love that Moses had — the love of Jesus. That is the love that those who give this closing message will have. God is not going to send people to give the straight testimony, which does the final work of shaking the church, until they have received the counsel of the True Witness in their own lives and have this consuming, overpowering love for others. When we have that love, we are going to see backsliders reclaimed. We are going to see many who have strayed from the fold brought back to follow the Shepherd. David had something of that love. Saul was opposing him, chasing him, and trying to kill him. When Saul came inadvertently under David's power, there were those who suggested that David slay Saul. Did David do it? No. He said, "I will not put forth my hand against the Lord's anointed." He had something of this love we are studying. Oh, let us pray for that love, because those who have that love have the pure gold, the true gold, and that is riches of the greatest value.

There are those who say that the message to the Laodiceans shows that there is no future for Laodicea. I don't find it so.

> As many as I love, I rebuke and chasten: be zealous therefore, and repent. Revelation 3:19.

If the condition were hopeless, God would not say "repent." No. It is to those He loves that He sends this message. It is a message of earnest plea to return. Thank God, our condition is not hopeless, if we will listen to the True Witness. Notice in *Testimonies for the Church*, Volume 1, page 143: "Oh, how precious was this promise, as it was shown to me in vision! 'I will come in to him, and will sup with him, and he with Me.'

Oh, the love, the wondrous love of God! After all our lukewarmness and sins, He says: 'Return unto Me, and I will return unto thee, and will heal all thy backslidings.' This was repeated by the angel a number of times." That is God's message of encouragement and comfort to His people. He is going to heal our backslidings. Thank the Lord for His tender patience. If we will enter in with all our hearts, be zealous, and repent, then the glorious promise:

> To him that overcometh will I grant to sit with Me in My throne, even as I also overcame, and am set down with My Father in His throne. Revelation 3:21.

That is the promise to those who come up to every point and stand every test, and overcome, be the price what it may. If you and I are willing, we can accept the counsel of the True Witness. Individually, we can seek for this gold of faith and love, this white raiment of perfect character, and this eyesalve of spiritual discernment. Individually, we can give ourselves to prayer, to seek God for victory. Individually, we can exalt the standard in our own lives. And as we do, there will come a revival of the straight testimony within the church. There will follow the great shaking which we are now entering upon. We will see it in its fullness. Then will come the latter rain, the loud cry, the finishing of the work, and the glorious appearing of Christ our Saviour.

CLEANSING OF THE TEMPLES

In Revelation 5:13 is the picture of a clean universe. John says: "And every creature which is in heaven, and on the earth, and under the earth, and such as are in the sea, and all that are in them, heard I saying, Blessing, and honour, and glory, and power, be unto him that sitteth upon the throne, and unto the Lamb for ever and ever." Is that chorus ascending now? Is there a unanimous vote for God at the present time? No. What a babble of confusion there is in this world. Think of the sound of blasphemy, the sounds of revelry, of mirth, of anger, of passion, of pride. How the ear of God is pained as He listens to all of it. But, thank God, there is a bright view ahead. There is coming a time when, as stated in the last paragraph of *Great Controversy*, "The great controversy is ended. The entire universe is clean." I would like to have our minds focus upon that glorious goal, that certain future of a clean universe.

The problem in heaven was settled 6,000 years ago. The controversy was transferred to this earth, where it has been waged for all these millennia. But soon it will be over, and one beautiful symphony will be heard. Thank God for that glorious hope!

When Jesus comes, He is going to destroy the devil and all his works. Why hasn't He come yet? Because there are some conditions that have to occur first. God must have a people prepared, perfected, and ready to meet Him. The preparation of those people is the work of this message. Our reason for existence as a church, as a denomination, is the preparation of that people. Yes, that's true, and thank God that preparation is going on. But, at the present time, the church has not reached that experience where God can pour upon it the fullness of His Spirit. There is coming a time, though, when the church will be clean. God will have a people pure and true before the visitation of His judgments on the earth.

There will be among the people of the Lord such a revival of primitive godliness as has not been witnessed since apostolic times. *Great Controversy*, p. 464.

I want to see a clean church, don't you? Remember, we will never get a clean world until we first get a clean church. But something must come before that church is cleansed; the individual members must be cleaned up — have clean hearts. There are three conditions that God is waiting for, and in that order. When individuals get clean hearts, God will soon begin the cleansing of the church. And when He gets a clean church, it won't be long until this world will be cleansed and be a fit place to live in. That's all it takes, friends, these three conditions. Note that it begins with you, individually. Thank God, if you and I will get clean hearts, God will soon have a clean church, a clean world, a clean universe. It is important for us to understand what is involved in all these steps and phases. There is something very similar in all of them. That is what I want to study with you now.

Especially do I wish to focus our attention on these first two experiences — the cleansing of the heart and the cleansing of the church. First of all, in each case, the casting out of Satan makes it possible for the place he was cast out of to be clean.

When Satan was cast out of heaven 6,000 years ago, heaven was cleansed. When Satan is cast out of the church, the church will be clean. And when Satan is cast out of the world, the universe will be clean. You can never have a clean heart while the devil has a foot-hold inside, because Satan defiles everything he touches. And the church can never be fully clean, fully purified, as long as Satan or his agents have any place within it. The world must be delivered from every vestige of Satan's influence before we have a clean universe. Thank God, it's going to be true. Satan is going to be cast out of hearts; he's going to be cast out of the church; he's going to be cast out of this world. Praise the name of the Lord!

Before calling attention to the method by which Satan is cast out, and the part you and I have in it, let us ponder this central figure, the church, and the cleansing of it. When Jesus was here on this earth, He began His public ministry after His baptism by working a miracle at the wedding feast at Cana. Then He went to Jerusalem and cleansed the temple. John 2:13-17 reads: "And the Jews' passover was at hand, and Jesus went up to Jerusalem. And found in the temple those that sold oxen and sheep and doves, and the changers of money sitting: And when He had made a scourge of small cords, He drove them all out of the temple, and the sheep, and the oxen; and poured out the changers' money, and overthrew the tables; And said unto them that sold doves, Take these things hence; make not My Father's house an house of merchandise. And His disciples remembered that it was written, The zeal of thine house hath eaten Me up."

He showed a righteous indignation and authority such as the disciples had never before witnessed. And the rulers and the priests were astonished, that a young carpenter from Nazareth, with no badge of earthly authority and no right to teach or preach or to rule, had dared to come into that temple and teach, let alone order out the things He considered improper. But they couldn't help but respond with alacrity to His demands. They were surprised at themselves later as they thought it over. But when Jesus got through with His work that day, He had a clean temple.

Three years later, He came back to Jerusalem, just before the Calvary cross. He found a similar situation, only it was worse. He again cleansed the temple. See Matthew 21:12. Then what did He say?

> It is written, My house shall be called the house of prayer; but ye have made it a den of thieves. And the blind and the lame came to Him in the temple; and He healed them. Matthew 21:13-14.

He drove out the money-changers; drove out all who were polluting the temple, and then, with the temple cleansed, He carried on the healing program — medical missionary work.

Here's a statement from *Manuscript* 105, 1898: "There is a work to be done that has not yet been done. The temple courts are not yet cleansed as they must be before the work Christ did, after the cleansing of the Temple, can be done. Then all the sick were brought to Him, and He laid His hands upon them and healed them all." Will it be done again? Oh, yes! However, this says it cannot be done — that healing work, in the fullness and in the great magnitude that we would like to see — until first something happens to the temple. The temple must be cleansed.

Another statement is from *Testimonies for the Church*, Volume 9, page 228: "God's love for His church is infinite. His care over His heritage is unceasing. He suffers no affliction to come upon the church but such as is essential for her purification, her present and eternal good. He will purify His church even as He purified the temple at the beginning and close of His ministry on earth." God has said quite a bit about cleansing the temple.

> Just how soon this refining process will begin I cannot say, but it will not be long deferred. He whose fan is in His hand will cleanse His temple of its moral defilement. *Testimonies to Ministers*, p. 373.

> The purging and cleansing will surely pass through every church in our land that has had great opportunities and privileges, and has passed them by unheeded. *Ibid.*, p. 414.

All this has a very practical application. These statements teach us how to relate ourselves to the apostasy, the worldliness, and the luke-warmness that is all about us. These signs, instead of being discouraging, help us to realize that these tokens, these predictions, are about to come to pass. What need would there be for the church to be purified if all were well within her borders? What need would there be for One to come with a scourge of small cords, and to say, "Depart hence," if everything in the temple were proper and praiseworthy? Every evidence of lukewarmness, every evidence of worldliness, every evidence of apostasy, are but tokens that Jesus is about to arise and do what He said He would do — purify His church even as He purified the temple when He was here on earth.

Where do you want to be when that purging and cleansing of the church takes place? Do you want to be inside or outside? I trust you will want to be inside. But the only ones who can be in that experience, and continue through it, will be those whose hearts have been cleansed by Jesus. There must not be one impurity left in the heart. A pure church will be composed of pure, clean individuals. God is going to make a clean work, a thorough work. Oh, that we might realize that!

The medical missionary program that God gave His people to reveal the kind of love of heaven has sometimes been turned into just a money-making scheme. God is not in that type of work. He gave this people the medical missionary work to reveal sacrifice, to reveal love; yet today people are even boasting of the tremendous amounts of money that are flowing into the coffers.

Medical missionary work includes reforms of more than one kind. It isn't just health reform, diet reform, or dress reform. It is reform in sacrifice; it is getting away from this commercialism which is eating out the spirituality of God's people. Note this statement from Medical Ministry, page 131: "All heaven is looking on with intense interest to see what stamp medical missionary work will assume under the supervision of human beings. Will men make merchandise of God's ordained plan for reaching the dark parts of the earth with a manifestation of His benevolence? ... We are not to cover mercy with selfishness and then call it medical missionary work."

I strongly affirm that the term "medical missionary work" should never be applied to much of what it is applied to today. When the temple courts are cleansed, when this making merchandise of God's program of medical ministry is cast out, then the healing power of God will be poured out.

The cleansing takes place in other areas as well. From Fundamentals of Christian Education, page 174, "There is great need of elevating the standard of righteousness in our schools, to give instruction after God's order. Should Christ enter our institutions for the education of the youth, He would cleanse them as He cleansed the temple, banishing many things that have a defiling influence. Many of the books which the youth study would be expelled."

What does "expelled" mean? It means driven out, forced out, excluded. And if Jesus were to come to many schools today, He would force out the pagan, infidel textbooks which lead away from the fountains of living waters to the broken cisterns that can hold no water. But God says He will cleanse the temple. So there's no need for us to lose heart or to become discouraged. God will take care of it in His own time and way. From *Selected Messages*, Book 2, page 390: "There is no need to doubt, to be fearful, that the work will not succeed. God is at the head of the work, and He will set everything in order. If matters need adjusting at the head of the work, God will attend to that, and work to right every wrong. Let us have faith that God is going to carry the noble ship which bears the people of God safely into port." Sadly, however, in this hour of purging, multitudes of our dear people are going to be swept away like dry leaves in the wind. Just how will the cleansing take place in the church and in individual hearts?

> Only Christ can cleanse the soul temple. But He will not force an entrance. *Desire of Ages*, p. 161.

We'll further answer the question as we study how the cleansing of the heart and the cleansing of the temple today are different from what they were at Jerusalem. And in order to help us understand, I'm going to go way back to the cleansing of heaven 6,000 years ago. That's where this whole sin problem started. Satan peddled his pack of lies to the angels. The time finally came when heaven had to be cleaned out. How? That's what we're going to study. And as we do, we'll understand how He's going to cleanse the hearts of His people and how He's going to cleanse the church. We are told in Revelation:

> And there was war in heaven ... Revelation 12:7.

Had there not been war in heaven, sin and Satan could have remained there. A subtle philosophy exists today that suggests "peace at any price." Some believe that all controversy must be avoided at all costs. This is an idea from the devil, for he knows what is ahead of us. Continuing on in Revelation 12:7-9: "And there was war in heaven, Michael and his angels fought against the dragon; and the dragon fought and his angels, and prevailed not; neither was their place found any more in heaven. And the great dragon was cast out, that old serpent, called the Devil, and Satan, which deceiveth the whole world: he was cast out into the earth, and his angels were cast out with him."

Incidentally, were there very many angels cast out with the dragon? Yes, one third of them! There was a struggle. Michael and His angels fought. Jesus fighting? The angels fighting? Yes, they fought desperately to cleanse heaven of that awful thing called sin. And this church is going to be cleansed and purified as was heaven 6,000 years ago. God could have cleansed heaven by simply telling Satan to leave. And he would have had to leave. From Spirit of Prophecy, Volume I, page 21: "The great God could at once have hurled this arch deceiver from Heaven; but this was not His purpose. He would give the rebellious an equal chance to measure strength and might with His own Son and His loyal angels. In this battle every angel would choose his own side, and be manifested to all." Do you see the strategy of God, His purpose? Instead of pushing Satan out, He gave to the loyal angels the responsibility of expelling the fallen angels. He gave to each one the opportunity and duty of choosing one way or the other. Every angel was either expelled or helped to expel. That was God's way of cleansing heaven. Can you imagine what it must have been like? Those angels were friends; there were not any enemies among them up to that time. Can you imagine the heartbreak that must have come to some angel while helping to expel an angel that he had loved for ages? It takes strength from above for us to stand up and give the straight testimony when it cuts right to the hearts of people that we've loved for years.

This is how purification works in the individual life. Perhaps you're like many a soul who is waiting for God to cleanse him, waiting for victory over sin; perhaps it's an evil temper now and then, perhaps a critical spirit. Whatever the iniquity, you may say, "I wish Jesus would come into my heart as He entered the temple at Jerusalem and drive that sin out of my soul." You can pray about it, wish about it, and hope about it from now until probation closes; but if that's all you do about it, you'll be lost! You've got to go through what those loyal angels in heaven did 6,000 years ago. With faith in your heart, courage in your soul, and determination in your mind, you must push the devil out.

The expulsion of sin is the act of the soul itself. *Desire of Ages*, p. 466.

Many may say, "I thought Jesus did that. I'll just turn it over to Him." Can you do that without Jesus? No. No man can of himself cast out the evil throng that have taken possession of the heart. Only Christ can cleanse the soul temple. You indeed can't do it without Him. Be He won't do it without you. He does it through you. Whenever you get ready for the devil to leave, God is right with you, infusing His strength into your poor, weak will. If you believe His promise, just give the order for the devil to leave. Push him out, and he has to go.

You may say, "Oh, I'm so afraid, I'm so weak, and the devil has resisted me again and again. He hasn't paid attention before when I've told him to go." Perhaps you were trying it without God. You must have such a love for Jesus and such a hatred for sin that you'll tell the devil to leave and mean what you say. Our difficulty is this: Deep down in our hearts, so many times, we hate to see him go! Hate to see the devil go? Yes, that's our trouble. But when we want to get rid of him as much as those angels in heaven did, he's got to go. He's got to go from the heart, and he's got to go from the church, and he's got to go from the world.

Reading on in *Desire of Ages*: "True, we have no power to free ourselves from Satan's control; but when we desire to be set free from sin, and in our great need cry out for a power out of and above ourselves, the powers of the soul are imbued with the divine energy of the Holy Spirit, and they obey the dictates of the will in fulfilling the will of God."

Who is to tell the devil to get out of your life? You are! If you do it without God, the devil will laugh at you and mock you; but if you wait for God to do it without you, you'll wait in vain. Cry to God, plead with God, for "whatsoever things ye desire, when ye pray, believe that ye shall receive them, and ye shall have them." (Mark 11:24). That's faith. It takes faith to deal with the devil. And when you have prayed to God for victory, then arise in the strength of God and be free. Say to the devil, "Get out! In the name of Jesus! And I mean it!" And the enemy has to go.

> Resist the devil, and he will flee from you. Draw nigh to God, and He will draw nigh to you. James 4:7-8.

That's a glorious promise from God.

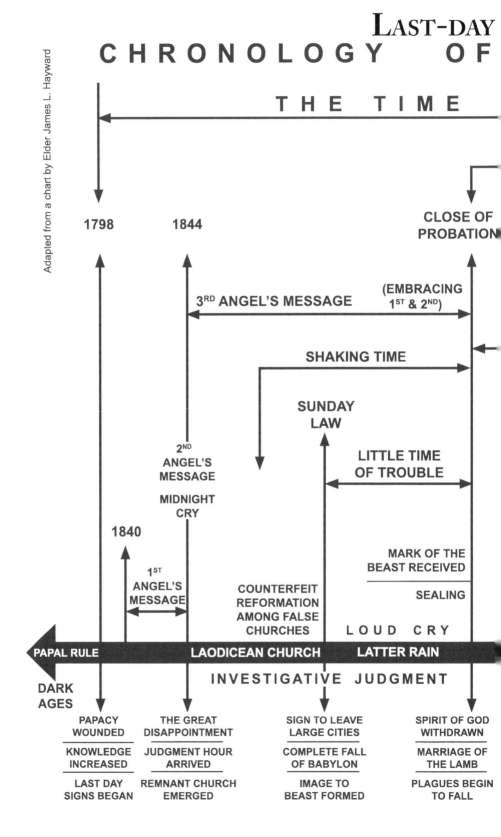

Adapted from a chart by Elder James L. Hayward

1798   1844   CLOSE OF
                                                            PROBATION

                    3RD ANGEL'S MESSAGE   (EMBRACING
                                               1ST & 2ND)

                                    SHAKING TIME

                              SUNDAY
                              LAW

          2ND   LITTLE TIME
          ANGEL'S   OF TROUBLE
          MESSAGE

          MIDNIGHT
          CRY

    1840   MARK OF THE
                                               BEAST RECEIVED

          1ST   SEALING
          ANGEL'S   COUNTERFEIT
          MESSAGE   REFORMATION
                         AMONG FALSE
                         CHURCHES   LOUD   CRY

PAPAL RULE   LAODICEAN CHURCH   LATTER RAIN

                  INVESTIGATIVE JUDGMENT
DARK
AGES

PAPACY WOUNDED	THE GREAT DISAPPOINTMENT	SIGN TO LEAVE LARGE CITIES	SPIRIT OF GOD WITHDRAWN
KNOWLEDGE INCREASED	JUDGMENT HOUR ARRIVED	COMPLETE FALL OF BABYLON	MARRIAGE OF THE LAMB
LAST DAY SIGNS BEGAN	REMNANT CHURCH EMERGED	IMAGE TO BEAST FORMED	PLAGUES BEGIN TO FALL

'S CHART
AST-DAY   EVENTS

NOTE: Length of lines are not to scale.

OF   THE   END →

THE   DAY   OF   THE   LORD →

**2ND ADVENT
OF CHRIST**

**HOLY CITY
DESCENDS**

REAT TIME OF TROUBLE →

**DEATH
DECREE**

**DELIVERANCE
and SPECIAL
RESURRECTION**

← TIME OF JACOB'S TROUBLE →

**RIGHTEOUS
IN HEAVEN**

SATAN COUNTERFEITS
SECOND ADVENT
(See *The Truth About Angels*,
pp. 273-275)

**FLEE TO
MOUNTAINS**

ARMAGEDDON

**WICKED
JUDGED**

**EARTH
DESOLATE**

**SATAN
BOUND**

SEAL ON WORSHIPERS OF BEAST	SEA TURNS TO BLOOD	ALL WATERS TURN TO BLOOD	SCORCHING SUN	DARKNESS UPON SEAT OF BEAST	EUPHRATES DRIED UP	HAIL EARTHQUAKES FIRE
1	2	3	4	5	6	7

1000 YEARS   ETERNITY

SEVEN   LAST   PLAGUES

MILLENIUM

**NEW
EARTH**

**RESURRECTION OF
RIGHTEOUS DEAD**

**RESURRECTION OF
WICKED DEAD**

**WICKED SLAIN BY
CHRIST'S GLORY**

**HELL FIRE
DESTROYS WICKED**

**SAINTS TAKEN
TO HEAVEN**

**EARTH PURIFIED
AND RECREATED**

Section 2 – Crisis at the Close

CHRIST FORETELLS THE SIFTING

In the great plan of salvation, there are two special crises — the crisis at the close of Christ's earthly life, and the crisis that comes at the close of the experience of the remnant. Between these two experiences, there are a number of most interesting parallels. The first five verses of Revelation 14 give us a picture of "the 144,000." Concerning them, it is said:

> These are they which were not defiled with women; for they are virgins. These are they which follow the Lamb whithersoever He goeth. These were redeemed from among men, being the firstfruits unto God and to the Lamb. Revelation 14:4.

What do they do? They follow the Lamb wherever He goes. Those who follow Him in heaven will first follow in His footsteps here on earth. We must begin where He begins in order to arrive where He has arrived. So it is concerning His earthly life. If we can parallel the experiences that He came down here to earth to share with us, there will be no question about sharing with Him those glorious experiences of the hereafter.

In this world, we look upon Jesus as a helpless babe in Bethlehem. We see the humility, the condescension, and we can choose to follow Him. In that humiliation? Yes. We see Jesus at Nazareth growing up as a child in a humble peasant home, bearing the burdens of daily toil, giving an example of patience and love. And as we see that, we can choose to follow Him there. As He goes to Jordan to be baptized, we can follow Him there. As He goes to Capernaum in His medical missionary ministry, we can follow Him there. But as we look at His life, we see Him come at last to Gethsemane; and there beneath the shadows of the olive trees, we look upon a great crisis. Shall we follow Him there? As we watch, we see the mob come. We see the Saviour taken and hurried to earthly courts, there to be abused, mistreated, falsely accused, and tortured. Will we follow Him there? We see Him led off to Calvary. We see Him nailed to the tree and hung up between the heavens and the earth. Will we follow Him there? Ah, if we will learn something of what it means to follow Him through those scenes of trial, we shall also share with Him the glory of the triumph, for triumph awaits those who follow Him. Triumph prefigured by His resurrection glory, and the hour of ascension back to the Father's house. All of these, in one way or another, we are to share with Him in this last hour.

Let me make very plain that there are some experiences that Jesus went through that we shall never in this life, or even in eternity, fully fathom. Jesus, as the infinite Son of God, as well as the Son of Mary, had many experiences as our sin-bearer, as the atonement for our transgression, that we can never enter into as He entered into them. In fact, many of those experiences He entered into in order that we might *not* have to enter into them. He was our *Substitute*. Concerning those, we need to seek to understand as much as is possible in our poor, finite minds. And concerning those, we shall study throughout the endless ages.

While all that is true, it is also true that there are many things that Jesus experienced that we can and will experience to some degree. I wish to study with you some of the parallels between the closing events in the life of Jesus here on earth and the closing events in the experience of the remnant — those closing events upon which we are even now entering. Of all the experiences in the life of Jesus, the ones that you and I most need to study are those that come right at the close of His life, because they have lessons of the deepest significance to teach us concerning the closing events of our lives here in this world. You remember this oft-quoted statement:

> It would be well for us to spend a thoughtful hour each day in contemplation of the life of Christ. We should take it point by point, and let the imagination grasp each scene, especially the closing ones. *The Desire of Ages*, p. 83.

Everything was at stake back in the Garden of Gethsemane and on Golgotha. And in this closing crisis, everything is again at stake. Back then, the entire universe gathered around to behold that great crisis. We are told that, today, the whole universe is watching with inexpressible interest to see the closing scenes here on earth in the great controversy between Christ and Satan. And the part that we are to play in this closing conflict is very similar to that of Jesus. So, with the deepest interest, we come to study these closing events in the life of Jesus, and to gather from them the lessons that will prepare us for *our* closing crisis. Oh, friends, won't it be a wonderful thing if the Father, looking upon us, can see in each one of us the image of His Son reflected fully? That is our destiny. For this we were born; for this we are now being prepared. And every experience that comes to us, under the guiding hand, is arranged by the Lord to develop in us the characters that will reflect the image of Jesus fully in the great crisis that closes the plan of salvation. "These are they which follow the Lamb whithersoever He goeth."

We want to especially notice the preview of the closing crisis that Jesus gave His disciples, and the preview that He has given us of *our* closing crisis. Jesus knew that His hour had come (John 13:1). Speaking to His dear disciples in the upper room, just a few hours before Gethsemane, He said:

> Now I tell you before it come, that, when it is come to pass, ye may believe that I am He. John 13:19.

He told them what was coming — the great crisis that was just ahead. Notice what Jesus said to Peter:

> Wilt thou lay down thy life for My sake? Verily, verily, I say unto thee, The cock shall not crow, till thou hast denied Me thrice. John 13:38.

Peter felt bad about this. In fact, he was offended. But Jesus was seeking to awaken in Peter self distrust. Christ gave this warning not only to Peter, but to all the other disciples:

> All ye shall be offended because of Me this night: for it is written, I will smite the shepherd, and the sheep of the flock shall be scattered abroad. But after I am risen again, I will go before you into Galilee. Matthew 26:31-32.

Jesus told His disciples that they would all be offended, that they would all desert Him as He went into that dark hour. But always in Christ's mind, as He foretold the future of darkness, was the glory beyond. That should be ever in *our* minds as well. The remnant church is to be brought into scenes of terrible darkness, experiences of sorrow, persecution, and sifting. But always in the hearts of those who listen to Jesus will be the certain hope of the ultimate triumph of the church and every true-hearted believer. Peter answered:

> Though all men shall be offended because of Thee, yet will I never be offended. Matthew 26:33.

Peter was sure that he would be true. When Jesus warned him that he would deny Him, Peter replied:

> Though I should die with Thee, yet will I not deny Thee. Likewise also said all the disciples. Matthew 26:35.

They were all sure that they would each be true. That only made more necessary the Saviour's repeated warnings, but it made them very ineffectual. Those words never penetrated to their inmost souls. We marvel at that. This wasn't the first time that Jesus had talked to His disciples about these trials and difficulties. Jesus was in Caesarea Philippi, many miles from Jerusalem, explaining to the disciples who He was. And after drawing from them the acknowledgment that He was the Christ, the Son of the Living God:

> From that time forth began Jesus to shew unto His disciples, how that He must go unto Jerusalem, and suffer many things of the elders and chief priests and scribes, and be killed, and be raised again the third day. Matthew 16:21.

Notice the setting of this. Jesus brought from their hearts the acknowledgement that He was divine and the Son of God. He acknowledged their acceptance of that truth. He said He would build that church on that great truth. Then, having made that firm and certain, He proceeded to tell them of the coming crisis. He said He must go to Jerusalem and suffer many things. How does Peter feel about that? He doesn't like it. His attitude in the upper room and on the road to Gethsemane reflected his attitude previously. He had never accepted deep in his heart the fact of the coming crisis. He never understood it because he never *wanted* to understand it. I wonder if you and I have come to grips with what is ahead of *us*.

Jesus made an earnest effort to prepare His disciples. But they didn't understand.

Jesus said unto them, The Son of man shall be betrayed into the hands of men: And they shall kill Him, and the third day He shall be raised again. And they were exceeding sorry. Matthew 17:22-23.

Jesus shared details with the twelve:

Behold, we go up to Jerusalem; and the Son of man shall be betrayed unto the chief priests and unto the scribes, and they shall condemn Him to death, And shall deliver Him to the Gentiles to mock, and to scourge, and to crucify Him: and the third day He shall rise again. Matthew 20:18-19.

Then came to Him the mother of Zebedee's children with her sons. And what did they want? They wanted the first place in the kingdom. With almost impatience and lack of attention, they listened to His description of the coming crisis. Their eyes were instead on the coming *kingdom*. They were sure that the glory of an earthly kingdom was about to burst upon them, and they were asking for the front seats. Nobody but Jesus knew it was His last night. In the upper chamber, what is the attitude of those gathered?

And there was also a strife among them, which of them should be accounted the greatest. Luke 22:24.

How it must have grieved the heart of Jesus; and He is grieved by such attitudes *today*. As we look at the whole picture, we see how Christ again and again tried to make two things clear: first, the coming crisis involving suffering and persecution and death to Himself; second, in doing that, His object was to help His disciples to seek and obtain the preparation that would enable them to go through that sifting without losing their faith. But we know the sequel. Here is a most significant statement from *Great Controversy*, page 594: "Before His crucifixion the Saviour explained to His disciples that He was to be put to death and to rise again from the tomb, and angels were present to impress His words on minds and hearts. But the disciples were looking for temporal deliverance from the Roman yoke, and they could not tolerate the thought that He in whom all their hopes centered should suffer an ignominious death. The words which they needed to remember were banished from their minds; and when the time of trial came, it found them unprepared. The death of

Jesus as fully destroyed their hopes as if He had not forewarned them. So in the prophecies the future is opened before us as plainly as it was opened to the disciples by the words of Christ." Do you know what is coming? It is your *privilege* to know. Thank God, those who understand the third angel's message *do* know. What we need to know is clearly presented. How thankful we should be, and how we should show our appreciation by applying that knowledge to our daily lives. In all our study of coming events, we need to be very careful that our minds are not diverted and thus lose the revelation of what God sees we need to know.

> Satan watches to catch away every impression that would make them wise unto salvation, and the time of trouble will find them unready. *Great Controversy*, p. 594.

Let's fix our minds most earnestly on that which is most clearly revealed. And if there are matters that are not so clear, let's leave them until, in the providence of God, they become clear as we go through the experiences ahead.

In Revelation 13:16-17, we read of a time coming when church and state are going to unite to enforce the mark of the beast, and that men won't be able to buy or sell unless they receive that mark. In verse 15, we see that a death decree will be passed against those who will not worship the image of the beast — something God expressly says that we must not worship. In other words, persecution was ahead of Jesus and His disciples back then; and persecution is ahead of the remnant that follows the Lamb today. Back then, Jesus said to His disciples that there was going to be a sifting. He foretold definitely that they were going to forsake their Lord because they had not prepared. And He has warned *us* that many are going to forsake Him:

> Then shall they deliver you up to be afflicted, and shall kill you: and ye shall be hated of all nations for My name's sake. And then shall many be offended, and shall betray one another, and shall hate one another. Matthew 24:9-10.

Jesus told the disciples they were going to be offended. He has also warned *us* that many will have that same experience. Was Christ betrayed by one of His own number? Yes. So He's warned us that those who are offended and leave God's people will betray them.

> And because iniquity shall abound, the love of many shall wax cold. But he that shall endure unto the end, the same shall be saved. Matthew 24:12-13.

We are going to have the experience of either Jesus or Judas. We can choose; obviously we can't have both. We will either be betrayed as Jesus was betrayed, or else we will act the part of the betrayer and join in the persecution of the remnant. Christ will again be betrayed, persecuted, mocked, derided, scourged, insulted, and spit upon in the person of His saints. How wonderful it will be when heaven, looking down upon this world, will be able to say that the remnant met their crisis as Christ met His. Won't that bring joy to God, the holy angels, and the unfallen worlds? Won't it anger the devil and cause him to pour out more of his fury? No wonder Revelation says:

> And the dragon was wroth with the woman, and went to make war with the remnant of her seed, which keep the commandments of God, and have the testimony of Jesus Christ. Revelation 12:17.

Jesus said that His followers would be sifted. We know what the sad results of that were. Likewise, there is coming a mighty sifting in the church. From *Testimonies for the Church*, Volume 5, page 79-81: "The days of purification of the church are hastening on apace. God will have a people pure and true. In the mighty sifting soon to take place we shall be better able to measure the strength of Israel.... The mark of the beast will be urged upon us. Those who have step by step yielded to worldly demands and conformed to worldly customs will not find it a hard matter to yield to the powers that be, rather than subject themselves to derision, insult, threatened imprisonment, and death.... In this time the gold will be separated from the dross in the church.... Chaff like a cloud will be borne away on the wind, even from places where we see only floors of rich wheat." Those who have step by step given in to worldly demands will find it easy to give up their faith and unite with the world. Keep in mind that it is the chaff that leaves and the wheat that remains. It is the false-hearted that flee while the remnant stands firm. The sifting results in purging the church of those who have long troubled Zion by their worldliness, their lukewarmness, their pride, their selfishness.

It will take more than desire to follow Jesus. To follow Him, we will have to share with Him in the preliminary experience. Otherwise, like the disciples, we will be surprised when the mob comes, and we won't know what to do. Here is another warning from Jesus concerning the coming crisis. It's found in *Great Controversy*, page 608: "As the storm approaches, a large class who have professed faith in the third angel's message, but have not been sanctified through obedience to the truth, abandon their position and join the ranks of the opposition. By uniting with the world and partaking of its spirit, they have come to view matters in nearly the same light; and when the test is brought, they are prepared to choose the easy, popular side. Men of talent and pleasing address, who once rejoiced in the truth, employ their powers to deceive and mislead souls. They become the most bitter enemies of their former brethren. When Sabbathkeepers are brought before the courts to answer for their faith, these apostates are the most efficient agents of Satan to misrepresent and accuse them, and by false reports and insinuations to stir up the rulers against them." That is what is ahead of us. One way or another, we will either be "the betrayed" or "the betrayers." We will either be like Jesus or Judas. We have our choice. We are making our decisions from day to day.

The closing scenes of Christ's life are revealed to us not merely for historical interest. And even though they are vitally important to show the great work that Jesus did for us, we are to look upon them with the deepest, personal interest, knowing that we shall pass through similar scenes and share some of those experiences.

GETHSEMANE

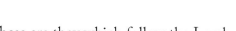

These are they which follow the Lamb
whithersoever He goeth. Revelation 14:4.

All through the universe, they go with Him. But first they follow Him here.

> We need not wait until we are translated to follow Christ. God's people may do this here below. We shall follow the Lamb of God in the courts above only if we follow Him here. *S.D.A. Bible Commentary*, Vol. 7, p. 978.

We noticed in our last study that, of all the events of the Saviour's life, the most important to us are those that are spoken of as "the closing scenes." In meditating on the Saviour's life, we are told to give special attention to those closing scenes. One great reason why we should be interested in those events is that we are soon to pass over similar experiences. We are soon to share with Jesus in the persecutions and trials and suffering and anguish concerning which He told His disciples. We are soon to pass through the sifting that they passed through. And we shall either come out victorious and triumphant, giving under suffering abundant evidence of the keeping power of divine love, or else we shall fail in the crisis hour. Just as crisis came at the close of *Christ's* earthly life, crisis comes at the close of *our* experience here in this world. In each case, it is the "crisis at the close."

The crisis of Jesus was the crisis of eternity, the crisis of the cross. The crisis which the remnant people of God are soon to enter into will answer forever Satan's charges and vindicate forever the character of God. God has chosen His remnant church to make that demonstration. And, in doing so, we shall meet the opposition that Jesus met. We shall go through the experiences He went through.

In our first lesson, we studied the predictions that Jesus made of His approaching sufferings and how He warned the disciples of the approaching sifting. The disciples approached the crisis hour with the warnings of Jesus in their ears, but with supreme self-confidence in their hearts. It was left with Jesus to act in harmony with what He knew was true, regardless of the attitude of others. That has great significance for every one of us at this time. Just prior to going to Gethsemane, Jesus had eaten the Passover supper and instituted the sacrament with His disciples in the upper room. He had conversed with them at some length around the table. And as they walked along the streets of Jerusalem and down across the brook and approached Gethsemane, He saw that beautiful grapevine which He took as the example of Himself and His followers, and from it taught those precious lessons found in John chapters 15 and 16. Then, kneeling with the band of disciples, He prayed that wonderful intercessory prayer recorded in John 17. But having thus committed His church to the Father, He pressed on into the Garden of Gethsemane to engage in that struggle with the powers of darkness which no one but Christ and His Father will ever fully understand. He desired His disciples to share with Him something of that experience. But, being self-confident and sleepy, they failed to enter in.

The picture of the sleeping disciples in Gethsemane has its counterpart today:

> By these sleeping disciples is represented a sleeping church, when the day of God's visitation is nigh. It is a time of clouds and thick darkness, when to be found asleep is most perilous. *Testimonies for the Church*, Vol. 2, p. 205.

God must find people today who will not be drowsy spiritually, who will press through the darkness, who will learn to pray as Jesus prayed, that they may be prepared to witness as Jesus witnessed. At the midnight hour, the mob came. The mob found Jesus prepared. When the clock struck the hour, He said to His disciples, "Rise, let us be going: behold, he is at hand that doth betray Me." Jesus was not surprised. He knew what was coming. That can be our experience. It *must* be our experience. But the disciples were taken unawares, although Jesus had warned them. They were not only surprised, they were unprepared. And although they desired to give evidence of their loyalty, before the night was over they all gave evidence of confusion and disloyalty.

The differences were made clear: Jesus prayed, but the others slept; He believed the prophecies and took action accordingly, but the others had their own plans and thought they were prepared for any contentions. Into one of those classes each of us falls. I praise God that there is still opportunity to change groups if we need to. We can enter in with Jesus, if we choose. We can go to Gethsemane and watch with Him. So let us look together at the experiences Jesus went through and see what we can learn about *when* to pray and *how* to pray.

If you study the divine commentary given us in that wonderful chapter in *The Desire of Ages* on Gethsemane, you discern that there is a growing crisis as the minutes tick slowly by. At the first of Christ's intense prayer, there is a longing in His heart that some way may be found that He may not have to drink the cup; but He comes out of the awful struggle with only one plea — that the Father's will shall be done. That is one of the greatest lessons in prayer that you and I can learn. Jesus was the infinite Son of God, and there was laid upon Him in the Garden of Gethsemane an immense load that will never be laid upon us. If it would be laid upon us for even one second, it would crush us. "The Lord hath laid on Him the iniquity of us all" (Isaiah 53:6). Hours before Jesus ever went to Calvary, He tasted the sufferings of death for every man.

Even in eternity, we shall know very little concerning that part of the Gethsemane experience. Christ took it for us that we might never have to know the awful gulf, the black dark pit into which He went. But while in that mysterious blending of divinity and humanity, as Christ took that infinite burden and suffered that infinite anguish, there were in His human heart the longings that would naturally fill our hearts. It was a longing that some way might be found that He might not be separated from His Father. Jesus didn't shrink from physical suffering to go to the cross and be nailed there. While it was a terrible ordeal, it was so small compared with the rest. But the anguish of the hiding of His Father's face in the dark hour pierced His soul. In the garden, He prayed, "Oh, My

Father, if it be possible let this cup pass from me." But He adds in sweet submission, "Nevertheless, not as I will but as Thou wilt."

It is perfectly proper for you to bring your wants and desires and longings to God. It is perfectly proper for you to say, "Oh Lord, cannot this be done?" But it is very appropriate in introducing any such request to say as Jesus said, "Nevertheless, not as I will but as Thou wilt." Unless that is in our prayers, we have not begun to pray as Jesus prayed. As Jesus continued, there came to His soul two things: 1) the certain conviction that there was no way for the cup to pass if we were to be saved, and 2) the certain decision that the Father's will would be His will — that He would drink the cup.

When we enter into a prayer experience with God, whether it's in asking for a simple thing we want, or whether it be through some great life-shaking experience in the crisis hour, we have not prayed with the mind of Christ until all we desire and choose is the working out of the Father's will.

Gethsemane was a garden in which there were olive trees and an olive press. For years and ages, olives had been gathered and put into that press that the oil might flow out. So in that press that night, the heart of Jesus was put under the great pressure of infinity that the oil of love might be pressed out to heal our wounds and nourish our souls. How wonderful it is that God permits us to share with Jesus, to some extent, the experiences of Gethsemane by going through similar pressures. Notice when and why Jesus went to Gethsemane. He knew that His hour was come. All through His life, Jesus had been guided by the prophecies. He was on time, all the time, because He was studying the time table rather than His own preferences or the suggestions of others.

At one point, His older brother suggested that He should go up to Jerusalem. They thought that He needed the publicity, and it would be good public relations for Him to go there. But He said that His hour was not yet come. But when the last Passover that He was to attend came, and His feet joined the pilgrim path to the city, He reminded His disciples of His purpose for going. Some thought to dissuade Him. But He knew His hour was come.

With eager steps, He pressed toward the place of sacrifice. That particular night, He pressed to the place of prayer that He might be ready for the mob. How did it happen that Jesus knew His hour was come? He had been studying the prophecies of Daniel 8 and 9 which said that the Messiah would be cut off in the midst of the week, and those three and a half years of the last week had come to a close. He also knew that, for 14 centuries, the Passover lamb had been slain on the 14th of Abib; and as the 14th day came, He knew that His hour was come. Before another sun should set, He — the Passover Lamb — would be slain. Knowing that His hour was come, He took Himself to the place of prayer. Thank God, He knew the time and what to do about it.

I wonder if we know *our* hour. I wonder if we know that the time has come for *us* to meet the mob, and that the little time that remains between now and the coming of the mob is set aside on heaven's calendar for one purpose — entering into the prayer experience. It will accomplish for us what it did for Jesus.

> We must pray more, and talk less. *Selected Messages*, Book 1, p. 122.

If there is anyone anxious to see the revival, this is the way it will come to pass. The influence grows. But remember that you, individually, are invited by Jesus to come with Him into the garden in prayer. You must not wait for others. Notice also that Jesus prayed in agony:

> And being in an agony he prayed more earnestly: and his sweat was as it were great drops of blood falling down to the ground. Luke 22:44.

That is something that we will never fully understand, even in eternity. Paul says to us:

> Ye have not yet resisted unto blood, striving against sin. Hebrews 12:4.

As far as I know, you and I will never be called to go that far in agonizing prayer, with blood actually being forced through the skin. But for each victorious one, there will be an experience of agonizing prayer. From *Early Writings*, page 269: "I saw some, with strong faith and agonizing cries, pleading with God. Their countenances were pale and marked with deep anxiety, expressive of their internal struggle. Firmness and great earnestness was expressed in their countenances; large drops of perspiration fell from their foreheads." I don't suppose that very many of us know first hand about that kind of prayer experience.

My greatest desire in this study is for each of us to grow in the prayer experience, that someday soon we may enter into the kind of intercessory prayer that will prepare us for the visit of the angels and the latter rain.

Jesus didn't *start* to pray that night; it was the *close* of His prayer experience on earth, not the beginning. The kind of praying pictured in *Early Writings* is not that of *beginners* in prayer. Long before this, they had a deepening prayer experience. Where are *you* in the prayer experience?

> And it came to pass, that, as He was praying in a certain place, when He ceased, one of His disciples said unto Him, Lord, teach us to pray, as John also taught his disciples. Luke 11:1.

So, how should we pray? Most of us know some of the following suggestions, and some may already put them into practice. But let's cover these simple, basic principles:

First — Have a *place* to pray. You may have more than one, but you never have *more* than one unless you have *one*. It may be any one of a hundred places, but have a place.

> Have a place for secret prayer. Jesus had select places for communion with God, and so should we. We need often to retire to some spot, however humble, where we can be alone with God. *Thoughts from the Mount of Blessing*, p. 84.

Let us never make excuses on this matter of our prayer experience, saying that we cannot pray because there are so many people around us, family or otherwise. If that is the problem, ask God to help you solve it — because your soul is at stake.

Second — Have a *time* to pray. The point made about place also applies to time: You may have more than one time, but you don't have *more* than one unless you have *one*. It is a wonderful thing to start the day in prayer with God.

> My voice shalt Thou hear in the morning, O LORD; in the morning will I direct my prayer unto Thee, and will look up. Psalm 5:3.

Daniel also found it necessary. Because he had so many burdens and problems, he had three special times for prayer. They put him in the lion's den for it, but it didn't break his habit. So, have a *time* to pray as well as a place.

Third — Learn to pray *aloud*.

> Learn to pray aloud where only God can hear you. *Gospel Workers*, p. 425.

I like the way that is worded. *Learn* to do it. We're in a *school* of prayer. The students of this school are going to endure. Praying aloud is one of the early lessons in successful prayer. You don't need to shout, for God is near. But speak *audibly*.

You may ask, "Won't God hear if I don't talk out loud?" Of course. God hears whispered prayers and even silent ones. And He knows what things you have need of before you ask Him. But prayer is not to inform God, for He already knows everything. He is waiting for us to open our hearts heavenward to receive the blessings He wants to impart. And believe me, opening your lips is a great help in opening the heart. Speaking directly to God helps you to feel that you are actually communicating with heaven. It makes it more real.

Fourth — If the mind wanders, bring it back.

> If the mind wanders, we must bring it back; by persevering effort, habit will finally make it easy. *Messages to Young People*, p. 114.

I don't know how many years it takes to accomplish that. But I am so thankful that I have a wonderful Teacher who is patient with me.

I am so glad He has given us these simple directions: first, a *place* to pray; second, a *time* to pray; third, learn to pray *aloud* where only God can hear you; and fourth, if the mind wanders, bring it back.

A tip for when praying in a *group*: Keep it concise. When we are all alone with Jesus, we can pray long and earnestly; and we need to learn to do that. But in *public* prayer, we need to learn to make our prayers *succinct*.

We have been studying the prayer experience. We have been studying what Jesus went through for us. He has invited us, as He invited His disciples, to share with Him in prayer. May God bless you as you enter the prayer experience as never before.

THE MOB

In studying the closing events of the life of Jesus, we have noticed how they are to be paralleled by the experiences of the remnant church. We have noticed the predictions of Jesus to His disciples of the coming crises of Gethsemane, the judgment hall, and Calvary. He clearly foretold the events that were to take place, and He urged them to unite with Him in prayer in preparation for that coming conflict. Likewise, Jesus has told the remnant church, through the Spirit of Prophecy, of the crisis soon to break. He has told us the experience of prayer that is necessary to get ready for that conflict, and He has invited us to watch with Him that we may be ready.

We have also found that to follow Jesus in heaven we must first follow Him here on earth, and that the remnant who will share a special experience with Him in the hereafter will first share special experiences of fellowship with Him here in this world.

In our last study, we noticed the Saviour's conflict in Gethsemane and how He took Himself to the place of prayer. He knew that His hour was come. Likewise, those who study the prophecies today will recognize the striking of God's clock. We should know that we are in the final hour, and just ahead of us is the crisis that the National Sunday Law will bring, the crisis that persecution will bring to God's church. And we should be seeking the Lord for that special preparation necessary to meet the special crisis. Just as the disciples slept in Gethsemane, many are sleeping now.

> By these sleeping disciples is represented a sleeping church, when the day of God's visitation is nigh. It is a time of clouds and thick darkness, when to be found asleep is most perilous. *Testimonies for the Church*, Vol. 2, p. 205.

So, while there are those who are sleeping, there must also be those who are awake and pleading with God.

Note again this quote from *Early Writings*:

> I saw some, with strong faith and agonizing cries, pleading with God. Their countenances were pale and marked with deep anxiety, expressive of their internal struggle. *Early Writings*, p. 269.

Thank God, there are some that are praying. You and I can choose whether we will be among the praying ones or among the sleeping ones. Confidence in ourselves can lead us to be so sure that we will face the crisis of the future that we fail to intercede and agonize in prayer to receive the necessary preparation. In this lesson, we are going to study the sequel of the Saviour's prayer experience and the sequel to the disciple's experience of sleep. Notice the answer to the Saviour's prayer. After finding a place a short distance away from the people, he knelt down and prayed, saying:

> Father, if Thou be willing, remove this cup from Me: nevertheless not My will, but Thine, be done. And there appeared an angel unto Him from heaven, strengthening Him. Luke 22:41-43.

Note the visit of this angel. This was the highest angel in glory, the angel Gabriel, the one who stands at the right hand of the throne of God. You can find the description of this wonderful visit in *The Desire of Ages*, page 693: "The worlds unfallen and the heavenly angels had watched with intense interest as the conflict drew to its close. Satan and his confederacy of evil, the legions of apostasy, watched intently this great crisis in the work of redemption. The powers of good and evil waited to see what answer would come to Christ's thrice-repeated prayer. Angels had longed to bring relief to the divine sufferer, but this might not be. No way of escape was found for the Son of God. In this awful crisis, when everything was at stake, when the mysterious cup trembled in the hand of the sufferer, the heavens opened, a light shone forth amid the stormy darkness of the crisis hour, and the mighty angel who stands in God's presence, occupying the position from which Satan fell, came to the side of Christ. The angel came not to take the cup from Christ's hand, but to strengthen Him to drink it, with the assurance of the Father's love. He came to give power to the divine-human suppliant. He pointed Him to the open heavens, telling Him of the souls that would be saved as the result of His sufferings. He assured Him that His Father is greater and more powerful than Satan, that His death would result in the utter discomfiture of Satan, and that the kingdom of this world would be given to the saints of the Most High. He told Him that He would see of the travail of His soul, and be satisfied, for He would see a multitude of the human race saved, eternally saved." Think of it — an angel bringing power from heaven to Jesus in that crisis hour. What a visit that was from heaven to earth! But it did not remove the cup; it did not take away the coming conflict; it did not hold back the persecution; it did not prevent Christ's suffering before the Sanhedrin and Pilate and Herod and at Calvary. Its purpose was to strengthen Him to bear it.

So today, as God's people enter into the prayer struggle described in *Early Writings*, pages 269-270, they too are to receive a heavenly visitation. There is another angel coming down from heaven with great power. We read about him in Revelation 18:1. And some wonder why his coming is so long delayed. It is not my purpose to study here all the reasons for that delay; but I do want to encourage you with this: When those who follow the Lamb follow Him to Gethsemane, and pray in their sphere as He prayed in His sphere, the angel will come today as he came back then. John says:

> And after these things I saw another angel come down from heaven, having great power; and the earth was lightened with his glory. Revelation 18:1.

That's what you and I are longing for. But remember, the agonizing prayer struggle comes before the glory. Before the visit of this mighty angel, God's people must enter into an experience that brings them to the place where there is just one thing they will want — the Father's perfect will. Humanity must be so blended with and subservient to the divine will that the remnant will be prepared to give an exhibition during their trial such as Jesus gave in His trial. And we are going to be tried in every way that men and devils can invent. Jesus was tried, and we will be too. To be prepared for that, we must have a blessing of a heavenly visitation such as Jesus received. But in order to be prepared for that, we must enter into the prayer experience. We must reach the place where our will is swallowed up in God's will, and our one desire is expressed in the words of Jesus, "Not as I will, Father, but as Thou wilt." Isn't it wonderful that God can bring us to that place?

We have noticed that the visit of the angel there in Gethsemane was not to take the cup from the hand of Jesus, but to strengthen Him to drink it. The coming outpouring of the Holy Spirit in the latter rain is not to take the saints out of the world of trouble; it is not to lift them above or beyond the possibility of suffering; it is to prepare them for the greatest ordeal of suffering that any human beings have ever experienced. That is the time of Jacob's trouble.

I want to study with you what happened to *Jesus* after the angel came, and what happened to the *disciples* after the angel came, and see if we can find the footprints that we must follow as we look at the closing experiences in Gethsemane. Luke 22:45-51: "When He rose up from prayer, and was come to His disciples, He found them sleeping for sorrow, And said unto them, Why sleep ye? rise and pray, lest ye enter into temptation. And while He yet spake, behold a multitude, and he that was called Judas, one of the twelve, went before them, and drew near unto Jesus to kiss him. But Jesus said unto him, Judas, betrayest thou the Son of man with a kiss? When they which were about Him saw what would follow, they said unto Him, Lord, shall we smite with the sword? And one of them smote the servant of the high priest, and cut off his right ear. And Jesus answered and said, Suffer ye thus far. And He touched his ear, and healed him."

John tells us that, as the mob approached Jesus, they fell backward. *The Desire of Ages* explains the reason. As the mob and Judas approached Him, the angel who had just ministered to Christ passed between the Saviour and the mob. As his glory was revealed, the whole host fell. It was apparent that Jesus could have escaped, and the disciples thought that was the purpose of the manifestation of glory. But Jesus knew better. As the glory abated, Judas started up. Think of the stubbornness and selfishness of that wicked heart. With all the manifestation of divine glory, the one thing that his mind was intent upon was carrying out the plan he had arranged, to come up and kiss Jesus and thus betray Him to His murderers. What an exhibition of sin. How realistically it puts before us the fact that there is nothing that divine love can do to reach the impenitent heart.

Notice the infinite love of Jesus. He allowed the traitor's kiss. He didn't push off the man that had betrayed Him for 30 pieces of silver. He only asked, "Friend, wherefore art thou come?" adding with trembling voice, "Judas, betrayest thou the Son of man with a kiss?" But Judas was unmoved. He threw his arms around Jesus and kissed Him, appearing to weep as in sympathy with His plight. We better get ready for such scenes. We have been told that there will be some like Judas who will betray their brethren. We know not who they are. Unless we enter into the experience that *Jesus* had, we are in great danger of entering into the experience that *Judas* had. Unless we are willing to reveal the great love of *Jesus*, we shall eventually reveal the greed and selfishness of *Judas*.

One of the great reasons Judas betrayed the Saviour was he decided to teach Christ a lesson. He thought that he had not been listened to sufficiently. He thought that his plans and suggestions were not given due weight. And if any of you are tempted along those lines, I plead with you, stop right where you are. If there has ever been allowed for a moment one little thought of bitterness in your heart because your plans were not accepted, your ideas listened to, your suggestions carried out, beware.

If ideas and suggestions are born of faith and love, they need no bitterness to enforce them. Faith and love can rest in the arms of Christ. Jesus endured with patience many delays. And at the close of His instructions to His disciples, He said, "I have yet many things to say unto you, but you cannot bear them now." He, the Teacher, had the disappointment many times of seeing His instructions not carried out, but it never made Him bitter. He never brooded over dark thoughts. But Judas did. So as we approach the crisis of the remnant church, there will be those who have, for one reason or another, become offended. Oh, that God may help us now, that every root of bitterness may be discovered and taken out, and with humility and love we may so place ourselves in the hands of Christ that we will be willing, like Him, to suffer (and *unwilling* to be used to cause others to suffer).

The love of Jesus in the garden, even with all that was going on, saw the man with the wounded ear — the ear that had been cut off by Peter

— and Jesus put forth His hand and restored that ear. That was the last miracle of healing that Jesus ever did in His life on earth.

That brings us to the study of another character in this great drama — Peter. He was not like Judas, but he failed in Gethsemane. And before the night was over, he dealt to the Saviour's heart a deeper wound than did Judas. The denial pierced the Saviour's soul more than the betrayal. This illustrates that there is more than one route to failure, more than one way to be defeated, more than one sin that leads to disaster in the crisis hour. Peter's failure came not from some deep-seated animosity toward Jesus; he needed to be converted deep down in his soul. Christ had warned him of that a few hours before. But instead of accepting the warning, Peter was offended. And when the crisis hour came, and he was awakened from sleep, Peter rose to the emergency and got out a sword and started using it in defense of Jesus. He was surprised and disappointed and offended that Jesus, instead of appreciating it, reproved him and undid his work by healing the man that Peter had wounded. When Peter was filled with fear as he saw Jesus allowing Himself to be bound and carried off by the mob, he was the one who suggested to the other disciples that they had just as well save themselves. Judas led the mob that took the Saviour. Peter led the group that fled away from the Saviour in the crisis hour.

In the coming crisis, there will be those like Judas and those like Peter. When the persecution breaks, when the National Sunday Law is passed, and when people are being put in prison, there will be those who will put up a great fight as Peter did. But their *fight* will only be the prelude to their *flight*. That thought should cause a deep searching of our souls. Reading from *Testimonies for the Church*, Volume 6, starting on page 400: "As trials thicken around us, both separation and unity will be seen in our ranks. Some who are now ready to take up weapons of warfare will in times of real peril make it manifest that they have not built upon the solid rock; they will yield to temptation. Those who have had great light and precious privileges, but have not improved them, will, under one pretext or another, go out from us. Not having received the love of the truth, they will be taken in the delusions of the enemy; they will give heed to seducing spirits and doctrines of devils, and will depart from the faith." All the disciples of Jesus were ready to defend Him and stand by Him loyally when the crisis broke. But not long afterward, He was standing alone. He had foretold this terrible sifting. That very evening, on the way to the garden, Christ had said to this very band of men:

> Behold, the hour cometh, yea, is now come, that ye shall be scattered, every man to his own, and shall leave Me alone: and yet I am not alone, because the Father is with Me. John 16:32.

Somewhere between now and the coming of the Lord, each in the remnant will be tested all alone. There will be times when we will be comforted by the fellowship of friends and prayers of our brethren. But somewhere between now and translation day, you will stand as Jesus stood — all alone. Would it be a good thing to learn to stand alone now? Might it be in the providence of God if sometimes we are placed in circumstances where to stand for conscience means to stand all alone? In view of this coming crisis, how shall we train the Daniels and Esthers of this last generation? Will the youth in your sphere of influence be prepared to stand all alone?

This leads us back to where we closed our last study. We need to learn to pray as Jesus prayed. Then we shall be able to witness as He witnessed. Although He had never failed once in all His earthly life, and had a deep experience with God, He dared not trust Himself to meet the mob at midnight with just an ordinary preparation. He prayed. The prayer experience He had those three hours in Gethsemane was simply the capstone to a whole life of prayer. Unless you and I have something on which to place the final stone in our prayer experience, we will not know how to pray any more than those disciples knew.

As we think on how Jesus stood in Gethsemane when the mob came, and why He stood calm, self-possessed, and loving, and as we think on how the disciples failed and why, surely we want to learn more about how to pray as Jesus prayed.

I want to study a few more points about prayer. In our last study, the points on prayer given belong to the *beginning* of the prayer experience — "the basics."

The next step is to begin to pray more earnestly and effectually than we have prayed before. And if we will learn the science of prayer, and keep applying that science day by day, Jesus will see to it that by the time the mob appears, we will have learned our lesson and have the glory that strengthened our Saviour in that crisis hour. As we think of Jesus in Gethsemane, the angel coming with glory, and the mob coming with shame in persecution, we think of what is ahead for us. There is a little statement that is so big in meaning that I want to share it with you. It's found in *Testimonies for the Church*, Volume 9, page 16: "It is impossible to give any idea of the experience of the people of God who shall be alive upon the earth when celestial glory and a repetition of the persecutions of the past are blended. They will walk in the light proceeding from the throne of God. By means of the angels, there will be constant communication between heaven and earth." The angel came, and the mob came. That blended experience is coming again. Would you like to see the angel? Then you must be willing to meet the mob, for they are both coming.

Great Controversy pictures some of the remnant of God being in prison cells, and angels coming with light to them — not necessarily to open up the gates or break the prison wall. There is going to be a blending of celestial glory and a repetition of the persecutions of the past. Do you see how necessary it is to reach the place where, like Jesus, we can say,

> The cup which My Father hath given Me, shall I not drink it? John 18:11.

That was what Christ was saying to Peter when He told him to put away the sword. He was explaining that he didn't need to fight or cut off people's ears, and that His Father had plenty of angels He could send, but that the Father had a *plan*.

Peter didn't understand. And unless you and I have learned to accept the petty annoyances and interruptions of daily life as permitted by a loving providence, we certainly will be utterly confused when the mob appears. Jesus learned those experiences in prayer, and we too are to learn in prayer.

To review, four basics of prayer are:

First — Have a *place* to pray. Select some spot, however humble, where you can be alone with God.

Second — Have a *time* for prayer. The psalmist speaks of two times for prayer, morning and evening. Daniel prayed morning, noon, and evening. In the chapter on Faith and Prayer in *Education*, it is suggested that children and youth find at dawn and twilight a quiet season of communion with their Father in heaven. And throughout the day we are to lift up our hearts to God.

Third —Learn to pray *aloud* where only God can hear you, not loud, just *aloud*; not just *think* to God, but *talk* to God. Learn to shut out the world and shut Jesus in.

Fourth — If the mind wanders, *bring it back*. If it does wander, don't quit or even get discouraged. That is just a challenge to do what this says — to keep the mind focused.

These four were outlined in Chapter 2, "Gethsemane." Here are two additional points about prayer:

Fifth — Mix Bible study and the Spirit of Prophecy with prayer. Take your Bible to the place of prayer, and perhaps take *Steps to Christ* or *The Desire of Ages*. Down on your knees, let God talk to you, and you talk to Him. This will help you with the problem of "mind wandering." Let the Lord talk to you through His Word — word by word. And having read a verse or two, close your eyes and talk to Jesus about it. In your own way, thank Him for what He did for you. Open up your mind to let God talk with you about what you've read. And if you will do that, you will enter into a rich field of prayer experience heretofore unknown. That is communion with God.

Sixth — Mix faith with prayer.

> For unto us was the gospel preached, as well as unto them: but the word preached did not profit them, not being mixed with faith in them that heard it. Hebrews 4:2.

Prayer and reading the Bible must be accompanied by faith.

> Therefore I say unto you, What things soever ye desire, when ye pray, believe that ye receive them, and ye shall have them. Mark 11:24.

Have you done that when you pray, or did you think it would be presumptuous? Faith is believing God. And Jesus tells us that, when we pray, we are to believe that we receive.

I think the reason many people find prayer so unsatisfactory is that they don't understand the different ingredients needed. Just as a balanced meal consists of more than a bowl of soup, there is more to prayer than just kneeling down and telling God a number of things that we would like to have Him do for us.

There are some things that Jesus went through in Gethsemane and Calvary that you and I are privileged to experience. To do that, we must know how to pray as He knew how to pray. Let us then dedicate ourselves, as never before, to learning the science of prayer.

> In the prayer of faith there is a divine science; it is a science that everyone who would make his lifework a success must understand. *Education*, p. 257.

Our success or failure hinges right on this point as we learn to pray as Jesus prayed. Thank God we are learning it.

THE TRIALS

J esus suffered alone, and we are to follow Him wherever He goes. "For even hereunto were ye called: because Christ also suffered for us, leaving us an example, that ye should follow His steps: Who did no sin, neither was guile found in His mouth: Who, when He was reviled, reviled not again; when He suffered, He threatened not; but committed Himself to Him that judgeth righteously." (1 Peter 2:21-23)

We want to study the trials of Jesus. We want to study the reasons for the repeated trials before the tribunals of earth. And we want to notice the parallel in the coming crisis of the remnant church. Like Jesus, we too will be seized by angry mobs. Like Jesus, we shall suffer the results of the combination of church and state uniting to inflict persecution. It is very evident that God permitted all that men and devils could think of back there in Gethsemane, the judgment hall, and Calvary. Why did God permit that, and why will He permit it again as the remnant come to their tests? There are reasons. One reason is to make a demonstration. As far as the death of Jesus is concerned, there are many ways in which He might have died. But there was a reason for all the delays and experiences. There was a demonstration to be made.

What is it that God wants to demonstrate? That divine love can be revealed in human flesh, forgiving its enemies and praying for its persecutors. He wants to reveal this, and it is more than a work of a moment. How long can you hold out? Did you ever say or hear someone else say, "I stood it as long as I could" when relating some experience? We will need to get that kind of thinking out of our minds. Concerning those who follow the Lamb in this closing hour, it is written in Revelation 14:12, "Here is the patience of the saints." As another translation puts it, "Here is an opportunity for endurance on the part of God's people." If you and I are ready as Jesus was ready, we will be able to give the same demonstration that He gave.

Notice the experiences that Jesus went through from His midnight capture in Gethsemane up until He was sent to Calvary in the early hours of the next morning. How many times was Jesus arraigned before earthly tribunals during those hours? Seven times — once before Ananias, once before Caiaphas, twice before the Sanhedrin, then before Pilate, then Herod, and back again to Pilate. In between these public arraignments, He was subjected to insult, abuse, and torture. Twice the terrible scourge was laid across His back, lash after lash cutting the flesh to the bones. The Roman soldiers mocked Him and arrayed Him in a purple robe, crowned Him with a wreath of thorns, and bowed before Him as if He were a king. The ignorant rabble, the rude mob, insulted Him in every way. There is a text in Isaiah that gives us a glimpse of some of the suffering of Jesus. Here is a detail:

> I gave My back to the smiters, and My cheeks to them that plucked off the hair: I hid not My face from shame and spitting. Isaiah 50:6.

They ripped His beard and spat in His face. They were rude, full of the spirit of the devil. And while Jesus was revealing God-like patience and forgiving love, the devil was giving through his servants the supreme demonstration of the cruelty and malignity of sin. It will be done again. Satan is studying your character and taking notes on what he finds. He is studying to find the particular thing that will make you lose your patience and lose your temper. With some, it is torture; with others, it is ridicule; for others, it is something else. Whatever it is, Satan is finding it out; he is laying his plans. And we ought to be wise enough to study our weak points as the devil studies them. Then get busy with Jesus and make our weak points our strong points, so when the devil finally comes he will view us with amazement, because we are a fortress impregnable to all his efforts. That's the way it was with Jesus. There was nothing in Him that responded to Satan's temptations. And if you and I will get into the experience with God that heaven wants us to have, we can come to our crisis hour and give the demonstration that God wants us to give. *Great Controversy*, page 623, reads: "Now, while our great High Priest is making the atonement for us, we should seek to become perfect in Christ. Not even by a thought could our Saviour be brought to yield to the power of temptation. Satan finds in human hearts some point where he can gain a foothold; some sinful desire is cherished, by means of which his temptations assert their power. But Christ declared of Himself: 'The prince of this world cometh, and hath nothing in Me.' John 14:30.... This is the condition in which those must be found who shall stand in the time of trouble." I want to stand, don't you? I want to get all the irritation and impatience out of me. I want to be able to meet the mob and give the exhibition that Jesus did. We need to know our Father as He knew His Father. Christ knew as He faced those persecutors that His Father would not allow one single blow or insulting remark without first weighing it to see whether it would be good for the plan of salvation. That was why Jesus rested in His Father's arms. All through that disgraceful farce of a trial, as hour after hour of torture went on, He knew that His Father was managing things. He didn't try to interfere or defend Himself. He didn't get angry or discouraged. He didn't wilt. He wasn't intimidated.

It seems that different camps of this world are practicing on one another. Atheistic communism and Roman Catholicism are engaged in a duel. One of the techniques used is "brainwashing." One of the great cardinals of the Catholic Church was taken by the communists, and was subjected for a long time to certain procedures which finally proceeded to wilt him. It is going to be a great surprise as the powers of this world, led by the devil, find some people that no amount of torture, physical or mental, can wilt. It will take a miracle of God, because the torturers of this age will have at their hand not only all the weapons of the past, but many new weapons of which we know very little. Thank God, we don't need to know all about it. But one thing we need to know is found in Daniel 11. It tells us the secret of the success of the Waldenses and others in the Dark Ages who gave their witness for God in those days of bloody persecution. This will be true again for those who stand for God in this last, crisis hour:

> But the people that do know their God shall be strong, and do exploits. Daniel 11:32.

What is the secret of strength? Knowing our God. So whether Jesus was meeting the rough rabble, the cunning priests, the vacillating Pilate, the cruel Herod, or those forceful soldiers in their work of torture and execution, He revealed God in the flesh to them all. That great mystery of godliness is to be demonstrated again in the remnant. God is to have here on earth a group of people who will make a grand demonstration that there is power in Jesus to make a man loving and meek and patient under the most awful circumstances. Notice what Jesus said to His disciples:

> Go your ways: behold, I send you forth as lambs among wolves. Luke 10:3.

Jesus was the Lamb, the Lamb of God. So He was before His persecutors. It is prophesied of Him:

> He is brought as a lamb to the slaughter, and as a sheep before her shearers is dumb, so He openeth not His mouth. Isaiah 53:7.

Can you do that, friends? There are some things harder to bear than the rude blow of the rough mob. To have people lie about you may be harder than to have them hit you in the face. Jesus had both. False witnesses were testifying against Him before the Sanhedrin and the court of Pilate. But like a lamb, He was silent — not through cowardice, but in calm courage. I will have to admit that I don't have meekness like that naturally. What about you? But I thank God that He has promised to get us ready for those experiences if we will let Him. He is getting us ready for those martyr days ahead. These words were spoken by Ellen White in the valley of the Waldenses — over there amid those towering peaks of the Alps where the martyrs for God had laid down their lives: "God does not give us the spirit of the martyrs today, for we have not come to the point of martyrdom. He is now testing us by smaller trials and crosses. And at times when it seems that the billows of temptation will go over our heads, let us remember that the eye of God is watching over us, and let us be willing to endure all the trials He sees fit to send." (*Historical Sketches*, p. 233) Children can learn arithmetic with pennies just as well as they can with dollar bills, can't they? It is the same principle. And you and I can learn to be patient and rely on God with these little trials and petty difficulties. We can learn to depend on Jesus and to reveal His love. And if we will learn it with small matters, God will help us carry it out with "matters of life and death." The terrible trials that are ahead can be met with the same grace that sustains us now in these little difficulties of daily life. Do you see how important it is to get the victory *daily?* For if we fail now, what will we do later? God will develop us for that later time, if we let Him.

We are going to be brought before the tribunals as Jesus was. Here is a statement from the *Review and Herald*, December 18, 1888: "It does not seem possible to us now that any should have to stand alone; but if God has ever spoken by me, the time will come when we shall be brought before councils and before thousands for His name's sake, and each one will have to give the reason for his faith. Then will come the severest criticism upon every position that has been taken for the truth."

Here is another interesting statement, this one from *Testimonies for the Church*, Volume 5, page 463: "The members of the church will individually be tested and proved. They will be placed in circumstances where they will be forced to bear witness for the truth. Many will be called to speak before councils and in courts of justice, perhaps separately and alone." If you and I believe this, what will we do? We will do what Joseph did in Egypt when he knew his family was coming — he stored up. And we should be storing up the Bible in our minds and hearts now, because they won't furnish us Bibles when they put us in the dungeon. It will be a wonderful thing if we can draw on the Word in our minds, won't it? Memorizing the Word is only part of it. Ask God to so teach us its meaning that, when the time comes when we are examined, His Spirit will be able to bring to our remembrance the truths and answer the questions that are given us. And if we are faithful in that, what is going to happen? Some of the great men of the earth are going to step out and take their stand right at that time. Regarding this time of testing when we are brought before the courts, *Great Controversy* states on page 607: "As the movement for Sunday enforcement becomes more bold and decided, the law will be invoked against commandment keepers. They will be threatened with fines and imprisonment... Those who are arraigned before the courts make a strong vindication of the truth, and some who hear them are led to take their stand to keep all the commandments of God. Thus light will be brought before thousands who otherwise would know nothing of these truths." I think that is wonderful, don't you? And it says:

When the final warning shall be given, it will arrest the attention of these leading men through whom the Lord is now working, and some of them will accept it, and will stand with the people of God through the time of trouble. *Great Controversy*, p. 610.

God is going to use some humble witness called before the court who will speak the word that will send conviction to some judge, attorney, legislator, governor, or senator. The seed that has been sown in his heart is caused to spring up in that crisis hour through the ministration of the Holy Spirit, and he will step out and say, "This is the truth and I am going to accept it." But it depends upon God's people making the demonstration, giving the evidence of loyalty and love — loyalty to God, love for His law, and love for people (even their worst enemies). Never must there be an angry word or sarcastic look; never should we take advantage of our opponents by some twist of a word; but rather we can give a sweet, calm, confident presentation of the truth. Again, we need to be practicing. God is furnishing us the material on which to practice. That is the purpose of daily life experiences.

Everyone is going to be tested, young and old. It states in *Testimonies for the Church*, Volume 5, page 525, concerning this matter: "The principles necessary for our youth to cultivate must be kept before them in their daily education, that when the decree shall go forth requiring all to worship the beast and his image, they may make the right decisions, and have strength to declare, without wavering, their confidence in the commandments of God and the faith of Jesus, even at the very time when the law of God is made void by the religious world. Those who waver now and are tempted to follow in the wake of apostates who have departed from the faith, 'giving heed to seducing spirits, and doctrines of devils,' will surely be found on the side of those who make void the law of God, unless they repent and plant their feet firmly upon the faith once delivered to the saints."

Are youth known more for wavering than for stability? Are there many who have the idea that young people have to come to a certain age and then settle down and become stable? The Bible does not teach that. Instability is not the experience that our young people are to have. Joseph was only 17 when he met the great crisis of his life. He stood firm for

God. Daniel was only 18 when he was ushered into Babylon with all its temptations, and made those decisions that established him forever as a witness for the King of kings. Jesus was only 12 when, in the temple at Jerusalem, He made it evident that there was just one motive that moved Him — to be about His Father's business. So, dear friends, we are to help children get ready for what is ahead. Here is a challenge to parents from *Child Guidance*, page 491: "Parents, ask yourselves the solemn question, 'Have we educated our children to yield to parental authority, and thus trained them to obey God, to love Him, to hold His law as the supreme guide of conduct and life? Have we educated them to be missionaries for Christ? To go about doing good?' Believing parents, your children will have to fight decisive battles for the Lord in the day of conflict; and while they win victories for the Prince of peace, they may be gaining triumphs for themselves. But if they have not been brought up in the fear of the Lord; if they have no knowledge of Christ, no connection with heaven, they will have no moral power, and they will yield to earthly potentates who have assumed to exalt themselves above the God of heaven in establishing a spurious sabbath to take the place of the Sabbath of Jehovah."

Are you teaching your children to be obedient to you, and thus to be obedient to God? The real test of any obedience is when a child is told to do something that he would not want to do. As long as the thing he is told to do is something he wants to do, there is no test as to whether he is obedient or not. All ideas that would set aside the necessity of obedience have their origin in that master mind that persuaded one third of the angels of heaven that obedience to law was not necessary for angels. And the devil is still spreading those theories. Oh, friends, may we learn God's way in this vital subject. It was because Joseph had learned obedience with his father in the tents of Canaan that he was prepared to stand alone for God amid the corruption and in the terrible dungeon in Egypt. It was because Daniel had learned obedience in his home in Judea that he was prepared to stand for God amid all the vices and luxuries, and also at the threat of losing his life. Amid all those problems and experiences, he was true because he had learned obedience. Jesus is looking for some children today who, like Him, will learn obedience. Jesus at the age of 12 recognized His Sonship to His Father, but immediately it is added:

> And He went down with them, and came to Nazareth, and was subject unto them. Luke 2:51.

All through His teens and twenties Jesus gave an exhibition of loving obedience to those who, in God's providence, were over Him. We too have those lessons to learn. And God is looking for those who will learn the lessons and learn them fast. We are rapidly coming to an hour when, in the closing days of the harvest time, every plant will go to seed. Children in their teens will be manifesting characters of those much older. Even today, children are becoming old in sin at an early age. And God expects there to be some youthful Samuels and Johns today just as there are youthful fanatics urged on by the frenzy of the devil. It can be done. As the spirit of Satan can grip the hearts of children, so the Spirit of God can come upon them and cause them to be witnesses for Christ. While the children themselves must choose, most of them will go the wrong way unless they are trained to love obedience and to obey because they love. Parents must give an exhibition of love and firmness so blended together that there is no way to separate them.

So, as we enter the coming crisis and think of ourselves and our children being brought before the tribunals of earth, let us learn and teach the lessons of loving obedience. With the voices of spiritualism croaking and mumbling about us, God is calling for parents and children who will be the light of the world in this crisis hour. Joel says it is time to blow the trumpet and gather the people. The children are to be gathered along with the fathers and mothers as we seek a preparation for the day of God.

Let us allow God to do thorough work in our hearts. Put away every spirit of rebellion or selfish desire to have your own way. Jesus learned obedience by the things which He suffered. Every one of us also must learn it. Let each of us earnestly say, "Yes, Jesus, I want to learn loving obedience."

THE CROSS

L uke 23:33-37 says: "And when they were come to the place, which is called Calvary, there they crucified Him, and the malefactors, one on the right hand, and the other on the left. Then said Jesus, Father, forgive them; for they know not what they do. And they parted His raiment, and cast lots. And the people stood beholding. And the rulers also with them derided Him, saying, He saved others; let Him save Himself, if He be Christ, the chosen of God. And the soldiers also mocked Him, coming to Him, and offering Him vinegar, And saying, If Thou be the king of the Jews, save Thyself."

You and I are going to Calvary in just a little while. We are to go over the road that Jesus traveled. As I have pointed out, there is much in the agony of the Saviour in Gethsemane and on the cross that human beings can never fathom. There is also much that we can understand only by experience. Paul longed not only to know the power of Christ's resurrection but, before that, the fellowship of His sufferings. To the remnant church will be given the great privilege to drink of His cup and to be baptized with His baptism.

We have seen how Jesus, knowing His hour had come, took Himself to prayer in the garden. Likewise the remnant, knowing the time according to the prophetic clock, must take themselves to prayer, and must enter into the experience written:

> With strong faith and agonizing cries, pleading with God. *Early Writings*, p. 269.

We have seen how the coming of the mob found Jesus alert and ready while the disciples were unprepared. Again, the hour of persecution will find those who have pled with God and received the latter rain ready to meet the mob, while those who have slept will leave the church in the crisis hour.

Never forget that it is those who flee who fail. The remnant that remains gathers strength from the trying process, exhibiting the beauty of holiness amid the surrounding apostasy. And as Jesus in the judgment hall gave that supreme exhibition of meekness and love, so the remnant, in the closing hour, will reveal to all the world such forgiving love as the Saviour manifested.

Coming directly to the culmination of the Saviour's trial, we notice several details which are to be paralleled today. Let us think of what brought about the death decree upon the Saviour. It was a uniting of religious prejudice and bigotry with political power. That is what crucified the Saviour. The mob, influenced by the leaders of the Jewish church, clamored for the blood of Jesus. And we are all familiar with the story of how Pilate was drawn along until finally, yielding to their insistence, he signed the death decree. Read now from the book of Luke 23:23-25, "And they were instant with loud voices, requiring that He might be crucified. And the voices of them and of the chief priests prevailed. And Pilate gave sentence that it should be as they required. And he released unto them him that for sedition and murder was cast into prison, whom they had desired; but he delivered Jesus to their will."

We know how there is soon going to be such mass pressure that legislators will yield to popular demand. Do not think that this great persecution is going to be something that a few evil-minded individuals are going to put over on the masses. The world itself is going to crucify Christ afresh in the person of His saints. Notice this statement from *Great Controversy*, page 615: "As the Sabbath has become the special point of controversy throughout Christendom, and religious and secular authorities have combined to enforce the observance of the Sunday, the persistent refusal of a small minority to yield to the popular demand will make them objects of universal execration." Religious and secular authorities combine in this great persecution that is just ahead. They did back then, and they will again. It was through fear of the people that Pilate yielded. He was yielding to mass pressure.

> Through fear of losing his power and authority, Pilate consented to the death of Jesus. *Early Writings*, p. 174.

So it is written of today: "The dignitaries of church and state will unite to bribe, persuade, or compel all classes to honor the Sunday.... Political corruption is destroying love of justice and regard for truth; and even in free America, rulers and legislators, in order to secure public favor, will yield to the popular demand for a law enforcing Sunday observance." (*Great Controversy*, p. 592) Do you see the striking parallel? Pilate yielded to the popular demand and signed the death decree against the Saviour. So today, legislators will yield to the popular demand that the people of God shall be put under condemnation. As the people were stirred up by the religious leaders back then, so it will be again.

Note the argument that religious leaders used to bring to focus the thought that Jesus should be put out of the way. Caiaphas had what he thought was a great inspiration.

> And one of them, named Caiaphas, being the high priest that same year, said unto them, Ye know nothing at all, Nor consider that it is expedient for us, that one man should die for the people, and that the whole nation perish not. John 11:49-50.

Caiaphas put forth the thought that even if Jesus was innocent, His influence was unsettling everything; so it would be better for the nation if He was put out of the way. Notice the parallel in *Great Controversy*, page 615: "It will be urged that the few who stand in opposition to an institution of the church and a law of the state ought not to be tolerated; that it is better for them to suffer than for whole nations to be thrown into confusion and lawlessness. The same argument many centuries ago was brought against Christ by the 'rulers of the people.' ... This argument will appear conclusive; and a decree will finally be issued against those who hallow the Sabbath of the fourth commandment, denouncing them as deserving of the severest punishment and giving the people liberty, after a certain time, to put them to death."

What secured the death decree against Jesus is the very argument that is going to secure the death decree against the saints. My eye caught these words so closely paralleled in the experience of Jesus and the experience of the remnant. As Pilate finally signed the death decree and turned Jesus over to the mob, they took Jesus and led Him away to

Calvary to crucify Him. There is a little expression that gives a picture of the mob's spirit:

> With shouts of triumph they led the dear Saviour away. *Early Writings*, p. 175.

Have you ever been around a howling mob? Probably few of us have, but we will very soon. It is not a pretty sight, and it is a terrible sound. Those "shouts of triumph" are going to be repeated as the hour comes for the execution of the death decree:

> With shouts of triumph, jeering, and imprecation,throngs of evil men are about to rush upon their prey. *Great Controversy*, p. 635.

It is true that the remnant will not actually be killed as Jesus was killed. There the parallel is not followed. They will go through many of the experiences that Jesus went through, but the deliverance of the remnant will come just at the point of death.

The worst thing about dying is not to quit living. The actual expiring of the Saviour was a release from the awful anguish and suffering He had long been going through. And the agony and the anguish that the saints experience during the time of Jacob's trouble will be a far greater trial than the death of the martyrs. It is a fact that they will not be executed. But let not that in any sense dim the vision of the trial, the test. It will be a trial and a test greater than mere physical death.

We read at the beginning of our study that various groups of people united in ridiculing Christ as He hung upon the cross. The rulers derided Him, the soldiers mocked, and even the thieves that were hanging there on either side of Him expressed doubt. Others of the gospel writers tell us that the multitude that passed by joined in reviling the Saviour. In their ignorance, they thought that they had made a point and an argument. They thought that the silence of Christ and His apparent weakness proved that His claims were false, and that He was not truly the Son of God. But you and I know that it was because of love and pity that He hung there and bore all that abuse, and stayed on the cross when He might have come down.

The remnant is going to suffer in a similar way the howling of the mob and the jeering and imprecation. Notice this statement in *Early Writings*, page 283: "It was an hour of fearful, terrible agony to the saints. Day and night they cried unto God for deliverance. To outward appearance, there was no possibility of their escape. The wicked had already begun to triumph, crying out, 'Why doesn't your God deliver you out of our hands? Why don't you go up and save your lives?' But the saints heeded them not." These scenes may be much nearer than we think. But Jesus endured in an infinitely greater way all that we will experience.

When the angels heard the chief priests and the multitude deriding Jesus, do you know what they wished to do? Again from *Early Writings*, now page 177, "The angels who hovered over the scene of Christ's crucifixion were moved to indignation as the rulers derided Him and said, 'If He be the Son of God, let Him deliver Himself.' They wished there to come to the rescue of Jesus and deliver Him, but they were not suffered to do so. The object of His mission was not yet accomplished." Do you get the picture? Jesus was on the cross, the multitude urging Him to come down if He is the Christ. There was commotion among the angels. They wanted to go and deliver Him right then and prove His divinity. But the tall, commanding angel did not allow it. Notice how striking is the parallel down here in Jacob's trouble found in *Early Writings*, page 272: "Soon after they had commenced their earnest cry, the angels, in sympathy, desired to go to their deliverance. But the tall, commanding angel suffered them not. He said, 'The will of God is not yet fulfilled.' They must drink of the cup. They must be baptized with the baptism."

The next thing I would like to have us notice is the darkness that fell upon Calvary as Christ entered into the deepest and most difficult experiences of the closing crisis. There was a struggle of faith and hope. He seemed to be forsaken, not only by men but by God. There was no intercessor. A terrible darkness hovered over the cross and especially about the soul of Christ.

> He had not one ray of light to brighten the future. And He was struggling with the power of Satan, who was declaring that he had Christ in his power. *Testimonies for the Church*, Vol. 2, p. 214.

How did Jesus get through that struggle? When hope was gone, faith and love carried Him through — faith in His Father's justice, and love for the people for whom He was giving His life. And as far as His relation with God, He had to fight the battle by faith alone. There are a few words, again in *Testimonies for the Church*, Volume 2, back on page 210, which tell volumes on which we need to meditate about on our knees: "Faith and hope trembled in the expiring agonies of Christ because God had removed the assurance He had heretofore given His beloved Son of His approbation and acceptance. The Redeemer of the world then relied upon the evidences which had hitherto strengthened Him, that His Father accepted His labors and was pleased with His work."

At Jesus' baptism the Father said, "This is My beloved Son in whom I am well pleased." He said it again at the transfiguration. But there was no voice in the darkness on the cross. There was no dove that came to Calvary. There was no ray of light.

> In His dying agony, as He yields up His precious life, He has by faith alone to trust in Him whom it has ever been His joy to obey. He is not cheered with clear, bright rays of hope on the right hand nor on the left. All is enshrouded in oppressive gloom. *Testimonies for the Church*, Vol. 2, p. 210.

How did Jesus win the victory? By faith alone. Do you see a deeper meaning in Revelation 14:12?

> Here is the patience of the saints: here are they that keep the commandments of God, and the faith of Jesus. Revelation 14:12.

If we are to *keep* the faith of Jesus, we must first *get* the faith of Jesus. We must have it and hang onto it. I think of this statement in *Testimonies for the Church*, Volume 5, page 215: "Oh, for a living, active faith! We need it; we must have it, or we shall faint and fail in the day of trial. The darkness that will then rest upon our path must not discourage us or drive us to despair. It is the veil with which God covers His glory when He comes to impart rich blessings. We should know this by our past experience."

That's what took Jesus through. When did He get it? At Calvary? No. He got it at Nazareth and Capernaum. He got it in Judea and Berea. He got the pinnacle of it in Gethsemane.

You and I need to be getting an experience from day to day in knowing for ourselves the will of God and in knowing that God accepts us. We can't afford to drift along to the time of trouble without that assurance. If we go into the darkness of Jacob's trouble with a *prior* experience in claiming the promises of God's word by faith, we will be anchored and able to go through it without an intercessor. Must we stand without an intercessor through Jacob's trouble? Oh, yes. And as Jesus won the victory by faith alone, so in Jacob's trouble we must win the victory by faith alone.

> The season of distress and anguish before us will require a faith that can endure weariness, delay, and hunger — a faith that will not faint though severely tried. *Great Controversy*, p. 621.

> Those who are unwilling to deny self, to agonize before God, to pray long and earnestly for His blessing, will not obtain it. *Ibid.*

Friends, I pray that we shall understand that this is why time has extended — to provide an opportunity to have this experience. You and I have the key. If we will enter in with Jesus and have an experience in getting rid of sin, claiming God's promises, relying on the righteousness of Christ, having the burden of guilt rolled away, and receiving power for witnessing, these other events will follow in rapid succession, and we shall be ready for the home coming. Let us remember that those who *triumph* with Jesus will first *suffer* with Him. Those who follow Him in *glory* will first follow Him through *shame*. Those who share His *throne* will first share His *cross*. And before the cross must come the trial and the test. And before the trial and test must come Gethsemane. And before Gethsemane must come a day-by-day experience over a period of time to develop a character and a prayer experience that can successfully meet the crisis at the close. This is the message for this hour — the message on which to focus our minds. Let the winds blow as they may. Let Satan invent all manner of things to distract. We must fix our eyes upon our Saviour.

The first vision that was given to Ellen Harmon was given in December of 1844. She said she raised her eyes and saw a narrow path cast high above the world. On this path, the Advent people were traveling. Who was at their head? Jesus. From His right arm came a glorious light as He waved it over the Advent band. If they kept their eyes fixed on Jesus, they were perfectly safe. I think that is wonderful. Why do we need to keep our eyes fixed upon Jesus? It isn't just some figure of speech, some poetic arrangement of words. As no group of people has ever done in past ages, the remnant must follow the Lamb. And in order to *follow* Him, our eyes must be *on* Him. It is that simple and important. Let's keep our eyes fixed on Jesus. Behold the Lamb of God on the cross. Behold the Lamb of God in Gethsemane. Behold the Lamb of God in the experiences that prepared Him. That will prepare us for the crisis at the close.

Every dark hour is the prelude to a glory hour, and the *darkest* hour will be the prelude to the *most glorious* hour. Whenever we experience darkness, we are to say, "There must be something wonderful just ahead. God help me to pray through this dark experience, because there is a glory beyond." We must believe that and have it learned so well that we won't faint and fail in the day of trial.

One of the most important lessons heaven is trying to teach us is to accept the assignment from day to day. Oh, how much we could learn if we would just be willing to accept the assignment. But there is so much mental effort used in trying to *escape* the assignment and evade it, run away from it, or pass it on to someone else — anything to get *away* from it. God knows our human nature is like that. But Jesus went to Gethsemane to get that power from heaven that would enable Him to drink the cup.

Will you drink the cup? Will you drink the cup from day to day? Oh, I challenge you: Don't try to get away from the cup. It is the Father's hand that holds it.

THE TRIUMPH

Read Matthew 28:1-7. What a wonderful message, and what a wonderful culmination to the crisis at the close of Jesus' life. Dark was the hour on that preparation day as they nailed Him to the tree; darker it was as the sun was blotted out; and darker still in the hearts of His friends as the evening shadows fell and He was laid in Joseph's tomb. But before the dawning of that first day of the week, there came light more glorious than the glow of the morning sun, for the angel of the Lord descended from heaven, rolled the stone away, and called forth the Son of God.

Satan thought he might keep Jesus a prisoner. Men had thought that they might keep Him there in the tomb. The Jewish leaders had asked for a guard, and Pilate had consented. A Roman seal had been placed on that tomb. That band of soldiers was set to watch it day and night lest something should happen. But I want you to get the picture of how that looked to heaven. Psalm 2:1-4 states: "Why do the heathen rage, and the people imagine a vain thing? The kings of the earth set themselves, and the rulers take counsel together, against the LORD, and against his anointed, saying, Let us break their bands asunder, and cast away their cords from us. He that sitteth in the heavens shall laugh: the Lord shall have them in derision." It was impossible for merely seals and soldiers to keep the Son of God when heaven's hour came for His liberation.

It came to pass on the resurrection morning that Satan and all his hosts were discomforted. Those soldiers fell as dead men. And what had been thought by the prince of evil as the time of his triumph became the hour of his greatest defeat from which he has never recovered and never will. The victory was won and made eternally certain for the universe. And Satan and his hosts knew that their doom was sure. You remember the wonderful events that happened in rapid sequence. Jesus appeared to Mary, comforting her and giving her the message for the other disciples and saying, "Do not detain Me, for I am not yet ascended to My Father." You remember that trip up to the Father's throne to receive the assurance from the Father that His sacrifice and atonement was complete and accepted, and that His church would be accepted with Him. The heart of Christ was ever with His struggling ones below. After that, He appeared to His disciples, and on several other occasions during the 40 days, He spoke to them, teaching them the Scriptures. Then came that wonderful day when from the Mount of Olives He ascended, leaving them the parting promise, "I am with you always, even unto the end of the world." The angels, who lingered near, said:

> Ye men of Galilee, why stand ye gazing up into heaven? this same Jesus, which is taken up from you into heaven, shall so come in like manner as ye have seen Him go into heaven. Acts 1:11.

As He ascended and drew near the gates of the city of God, He was welcomed by the angelic host. Many angels were with Him. Many were within the city. There again, Jesus made His wonderful plea for His church. The angels bowed in worship, acknowledging Him as the Prince of life. Those glorious events which happened centuries ago are to be paralleled by a wonderful triumph that awaits the remnant church down here in its crisis at the close.

We have been studying the parallels between the remnant and the Saviour. If Jesus comes to Bethlehem, they come with Him. If He goes to Nazareth to learn the lessons of faithful toil and humble obedience, to the Jordan to experience baptism, to Capernaum in medical missionary ministry, they go with Him. His desire to preach the gospel to the poor and reveal the Father's love, all this is reflected in those who share with Him in this closing hour the revelation of the love of God to man. If He goes to Jerusalem, knowing that He must suffer, they go with Him. If He goes to Gethsemane for strengthening prayer to meet the mob, they go with Him. As through all those different trials and tortures Jesus exhibited the Father's love, so the remnant church will reveal the saving and keeping power of Christ as they witness before the courts, in the dungeon, and in every place of torture and persecution. That will be the supreme exhibition of God's love in this last generation. Oh, that God may prepare us for it.

As Jesus was finally given over to death, as church and state united, so today the remnant people of God will finally be placed under a death decree when church and state unite. As Jesus at Calvary went though those dark hours in which He wrestled against the power of Satan, so the remnant church in the darkness of Jacob's trouble will wrestle against the powers of darkness. As Jesus was without an intercessor, so the remnant will be without an intercessor through the time of trouble. As Jesus stayed His heart upon God by repeating the promises, and by reviewing the experiences He'd had heretofore, so the remnant people will by faith alone press their way through the darkness. In Jacob's trouble, the remnant will not die as Jesus died upon the cross. He laid down His life and went into the tomb. He did that as the atonement for sin. There are many things in the experience of Jesus in Gethsemane and Calvary that we are not called upon to parallel. The Sinless One has taken our place. He bore the burden of our guilt. Thank God, we do not have to bear that burden. Nevertheless, we must go through the darkness by faith alone, as did He. And as Jesus was delivered by that glorious angel that brought the summons from His Father there in that dark hour of the morning, so the remnant church will be delivered at the midnight hour as the voice of God speaks from heaven, and glory takes the place of darkness.

From *Great Controversy*, pages 635-636: "With shouts of triumph, jeering, and imprecation, throngs of evil men are about to rush upon their prey, when, lo, a dense blackness, deeper than the darkness of the night, falls upon the earth. Then a rainbow, shining with the glory from the throne of God, spans the heavens and seems to encircle each praying company.... By the people of God a voice, clear and melodious, is heard, saying, 'Look up,' and lifting their eyes to the heavens, they behold the bow of promise." They look up through the heavens and see Jesus there at the throne and they hear His request:

> Father, I will that they also, whom Thou has given Me, be with Me where I am. John 17:24.

Continuing to read in *Great Controversy*, page 636: "It is at midnight that God manifests His power for the deliverance of His people. The sun appears, shining in its strength. Signs and wonders follow in quick succession. The wicked look with terror and amazement upon the scene, while the righteous behold with solemn joy the tokens of their deliverance.... In the midst of the angry heavens is one clear space of indescribable glory, whence comes the voice of God like the sound of many waters, saying: 'It is done.'" What will be the results of that?

> And there were voices, and thunders, and lightnings; and there was a great earthquake, such as was not since men were upon the earth, so mighty an earthquake, and so great. Revelation 16:18.

Back at Calvary, there was an earthquake when Jesus laid down His life on the cross, and there was an earthquake when He rose from the dead. So there is to be an earthquake at the coming crisis hour. There is to be an earthquake that marks the deliverance of God's people. And it will not only be the deliverance of the righteous living at that time. Daniel, speaking of that very hour, says:

> And many of them that sleep in the dust of the earth shall awake, some to everlasting life, and some to shame and everlasting contempt. Daniel 12:2.

Jesus came forth from the tomb glorified. Those who have been sleeping in their graves, and are called forth, will come forth from the tomb glorified to hear God's covenant of peace with those who have kept His law.

Shortly after Jesus' resurrection, He ascended with the multitude of captives going with Him. And shortly after the deliverance of the saints, shortly after this special resurrection, we too are going to ascend. And as a great company came from heaven to welcome the Saviour as the time for His ascension came, so all heaven is going to be emptied to come down here and welcome you and me, and to escort us home to that glorious city.

Jesus is coming very soon. What is He coming for? He is coming for you and me. He said in John 14: "In My Father's house are many mansions: if it were not so, I would have told you. I go to prepare a place for you. And if I go and prepare a place for you, I will come again, and receive you unto Myself; that where I am, there ye may be also." The parallel experience of the remnant with Jesus represents the fact that Jesus wants His people with Him. The heart of Jesus is, in a very special way, set upon the remnant of this last generation. These are they which follow the Lamb in a very close fellowship. You and I are called upon to enter into an experience with Jesus closer than all the angels that have never fallen. Why? This generation is to answer the charge of Satan that the law of God cannot be kept. As Jesus demonstrated in His life here on earth that the law of God *can* be kept in human flesh by laying hold of the power that God had provided, so God is going to have a group of people down here in the closing scenes. The book of Revelation pictures them as "the 144,000." They have the Father's name written in their foreheads. They have the seal of the living God in their foreheads. They have God's will fully transcribed in their minds and lived out in their lives. Thus they are given the exalted privilege of going through these trials and tests to make the special demonstration down here.

For 6,000 years, Jesus has been the intercessor, standing between the human family and a broken law. But sometime before Jesus comes, He will have so developed His people that He can step out between them and that law. And the people of God will stand there so fully clothed with the righteousness of Jesus that the law can find no fault with them, and Satan stands viewing them as a fortress impregnable to all his delusions. To him, they are an incomprehensible mystery. Do you see that Satan will do everything he can to break them? Do you not see that he will use every effort to keep them from making that demonstration? Oh, I am so thankful that it is written:

> Here is the patience of the saints: here are they that keep the commandments of God, and the faith of Jesus. Revelation 14:12.

Patience means more than meekness. It includes that, but it means *endurance*. It means the ability to carry through. They have the same faith that Jesus had.

As Jesus was welcomed by the angels when He ascended, so God's people will be welcomed by the angels and the representatives of all the other worlds. And as all heaven was filled with songs of rejoicing as our Lord ascended in triumph, so the universe will ring from one end to the other with triumphant strains as God's people are brought home to share with Him forever the glories of eternity. Revelation 15:2-3 states: "And I saw as it were a sea of glass mingled with fire: and them that had gotten the victory over the beast, and over his image, and over his mark, and over the number of his name, stand on the sea of glass, having the harps of God. And they sing the song of Moses the servant of God, and the song of the Lamb, saying, Great and marvellous are Thy works, Lord God Almighty; just and true are Thy ways, Thou King of saints." Oh, friends, is it not a glorious hour in which to be living? Thank God for the privilege.

There is a very practical lesson that ought to come to our hearts as we view the empty tomb, as we think of the glorious triumph of our Lord over the powers of darkness. Shortly after Ellen White's visit to the Waldensian

Valley where she had gazed upon those great mountains and had looked upon the places where thousands of martyrs had laid down their lives for Jesus, it recalled to her mind the things the Lord had shown her about the persecutions, and also the approaching crisis of the church. She wrote about God's care for His work. Notice in *Testimonies for the Church*, Volume 5, page 754: "Brethren, it is no time now for mourning and despair, no time to yield to doubt and unbelief. Christ is not now a Saviour in Joseph's new tomb, closed with a great stone and sealed with a Roman seal; we have a risen Saviour. He is the King, the Lord of hosts; He sitteth between the cherubim; and amid the strife and tumult of nations He guards His people still."

If we will gaze upon these scenes, we will have a great deal of courage. We will be able to face all sorts of emergencies and disappointments without losing our faith and becoming depressed. Oh, that this faith may grip our hearts. Let us join our words of thanksgiving with the angels. It will bring joy to the heart of Jesus. Let joy and triumph fill our hearts as we face the coming scenes — the "crisis at the close."

If you would like more more copies of this book, or would like to learn more about Elder Frazee's inspiring 1,660 sermons in our archives—please use the contact information below:

WDFsermons.org
support@wdfsermons.org
1-800-WDF-1840 / 706-820-9755
P.O. Box 129
Wildwood, GA 30757

27521554R00109

Made in the USA
San Bernardino, CA
01 March 2019